# The Ethic of the Upward Gaze

# The Ethic of the Upward Gaze

## Essays Inspired by Immanuel Kant and Nicolai Hartmann

PREDRAG CICOVACKI

ST. AUGUSTINE'S PRESS

South Bend, Indiana

Manufactured in the United States of America.

1  2  3  4  5  6  29  28  27  26  25  24

**Library of Congress Control Number: 2024940228**

Paperback ISBN: 978-1-58731-243-4

∞ The paper used in this publication meets the minimum
requirements of the American National Standard for Information Sciences –
Permanence of Paper for Printed Materials, ANSI Z39.48-1984.

St. Augustine's Press
www.staugustine.net

To Bogoljub Šijaković,
who led me to lift my gaze upward

"All other creatures look down toward the earth,
but man was given a face
so that he might turn his eyes toward the stars
and gaze upon the sky."
Ovid, *Metamorphoses*

# Table of Contents

# Preface

From the first year of my philosophical studies until the present, my main teachers and inspirations have been Immanuel Kant (1724–1804) and Nicolai Hartmann (1882–1950). Both Kant and Hartmann developed their philosophy in the spirit of the *philosophia perennis*. For both, the question of what it means to live like a human being was their central focus, throughout their numerous works in metaphysics, epistemology, and other branches of philosophy. Both understood ethics as having a transformative power, guiding us toward becoming as good as we can possibly be. Throughout the forty years of my philosophical career, these have been my primary orientations in philosophy and ethics as well.

My years of "apprenticeship" were mostly spent wrestling with Kant's *Critique of Pure Reason*, before I moved to other aspects of Kant's philosophical opus, primarily his ethics. Altogether, a good twenty years of my life were devoted to mastering Kant's philosophy. Though I have never lost my respect for Kant, my attitude toward his philosophy has shifted from one of adoration to a more critical stance. While there is much to learn from Kant, there are also plenty of his inadequacies in his work, on which we must improve.

My attitude toward Hartmann, by contrast, has remained one of admiration. Though his works have never been on my central bookshelf by my desk, they are still just an arm's reach away. My own views are much closer to Hartmann's than they are to Kant's, and I have always felt that, with Hartmann, the task is to build on his insights and develop them further, rather than to correct his shortcomings. This collection offers several ideas about directions in which such developments could continue. The essays collected here have been published before, over the last twenty years, in various journals, or as chapters in books. They were published initially as scholarly papers, with all the references and technical jargon needed for such works. I present them here in the form of essays: most are shortened a bit, with scholarly references deleted, and the technical jargon replaced by ordinary phrases that make them more accessible to a general audience. This way, the central ideas take precedence over demonstration of scholarly erudition.

These essays explore ideas relating to the suffocating and hope-crushing atmosphere of negativity and disorientation in the contemporary world. The message of this collection is that, if we dare to open our eyes and our hearts, we can find that there is much in ourselves and the world that deserves our reverence and our loving gaze. It is not too late to recall that besides the natural and the social worlds, there is yet another order of being: the spiritual. And without a connection with this spiritual order, we cannot experience our humanity at its best.

# Introduction: Vision and Ethos in Morality

Kant and Hartmann share a belief that is less common than it once was: that the aim of morality is to guide us toward becoming the best version of ourselves. Morality is not the same as prudence, nor is it a utilitarian calculus about what actions lead to our advantage. Yes, we do need to see what is in front of us, and handle what demands our immediate attention, in accordance with the rules endorsed by our societies. We also need to secure our existence as well as the material flourishing of ourselves and those who depend on us. But focusing exclusively on such issues deflects our consciousness from the high road of morality.

This high road of morality requires that we approach even those practical tasks with a sensibility that is only possible if we maintain an upward gaze. This entails fixing our attention on an order of things of a different origin and validity than the natural and the social. Following that road, we find ourselves at the threshold that both divides and connects what we, in our inadequate language, attempt to capture by the contrasting phrases: instrumental and intrinsic, relative and absolute, visible and invisible, finite and infinite, profane and sacred. In addition to our excessive pragmatism, which leads to what T. S. Eliot terms a "wasteland," we also are capable of experiencing what the poet refers to as "the points of intersection of the timelessness with time." Such interactions are not discoverable by either our pragmatic pursuits or by science. We can access them as rational beings (Kant's perspective) and as spiritual beings (Hartmann's perspective) who can lift our gaze toward truth, goodness, and beauty.

Both Kant and Hartmann accept that there is a gap between what is and what could and should be. No merely factual account can reveal a vision of what human beings could be at our very best. This vision is accepted on faith. Kant acknowledges that explicitly in the *Critique of Pure Reason* when he says that he had to limit knowledge in order to leave room for faith. Hartmann goes even further in his *Ethics,* declaring that such faith is not a matter of our voluntary decisions; it is more basic, more fundamental for everything we do. That faith in something higher and better is revealed in human interactions, mostly in moments of intense love, suffering, or joy, when various planes of existence clash and intertwine with each other. In such moments we can either look down or we can turn our gaze upward: we can become resigned, and lose faith, or we can find in faith our inspiration to do what we did not even know we were capable of doing. Through faith, we feel the allure of higher values, are drawn toward a richer and better world, and become convinced that the spirit can—and should—inform and guide matter. Morality, then, is not primarily oriented toward material or natural goods we desire, nor toward socially regulated rights. It is value-based and value-oriented, insofar as it leads us to choose which values will guide us toward becoming our best.

Kant and Hartmann disagree, however, about what "our best" might be, and even more about the path that can lead us to it. For Kant, this is tied to rationality; rationality and morality are two aspects of the same orientation. They elevate us above the natural and social worlds, as well as above the individually unique and historically contingent. They guide us toward becoming members of the "kingdom of noumenal beings."

Hartmann rightly considers this view as inadequate, as it ignores both the complexity of our nature and the richness of the world. Our emotions and intuitions are as much a part of us—and of what is best in us—as rationality is. Our natural side should not be repressed, but should be integrated into our overall being, as our uniqueness must be respected as well as our general humanity. What we aim to be, what our moral vision inspires us to become, is more complete beings with a variety of interests and aspirations. If there must be one word to mark our moral vision, it should be "spiritual" rather than "rational." The spiritual is based, not on authority or legislation, but on what connects and integrates. Guided by what Hartmann calls "emotional intelligence," the spiritual within us orients us toward the highest cognitive, moral, and aesthetic values and allows us to embrace the vast varieties of human experiences, including those we call religious.

Another way to explain the difference between Kant and Hartmann would be in terms of the distinction between realism and idealism. The cultural history of Western civilization can be viewed as a seesaw back and

2

forth between realism and idealism: first one dominates, then the other, and their hierarchical ranking has shifted numerous times. Hartmann, in principle, rejects the restrictive "either X or Y" thinking in favor of the integrative "both X and Y." Kant's vision of a morality that leads us toward the best we could be is an idealist one, as is Hartmann's. But Kant's realism is so vague that it leaves us disoriented, with no firm ground on which to anchor that idealism. For Kant, appearances are not the same as things in themselves, but we cannot know what things in themselves are. Thus, we cannot know what is real in any robust sense of that word. This is why Kant's ethics of the categorical imperative and the moral law sounds so abstract: they remain disconnected from our concrete lives.

The word "concrete" originally meant something connected, or things growing together. Hartmann is right to argue that everything that is real is concrete, intimately interconnected with the multiplicity of other things in the course of time, yet also individual and unique. The spirit itself is something real, emerging out of the other concrete layers of the universe: the immaterial, the organic, and the psychic. The spiritual, for Hartmann, is the highest level of the real world known to us, and is oriented toward the ideal world of values. It does not descend from heaven but, like a lotus flower, grows up from the muddy waters of reality; the spirit is the bouquet of the real world, not its negation or abrogation.

When it comes to morality, Hartmann believes that our vision of how to aspire toward the best requires something that is missing in Kant. This missing element can be called "ethos" —the word from which we derive "ethics." Ethos is, on the surface, simply the customary morality by which human beings live in their society for a prolonged period of time. Taken in that sense, the ethos of one group of people can be very different from that of another, a fact that prompted not only the ancient Sophists but also their later followers to maintain that all morality is conventional. Socrates and Plato opposed that line of thinking, and so does Hartmann. He treats the word "ethos" in a deeper sense, relating to the core of human moral behavior. What Hartmann elucidates is neither conventional nor particular to one group of people. In the ethos of all human beings, Hartmann discerns one fundamental and consistent value: trust. He compares trust with the solid earth under our feet, which we depend on for every step we take in life; it is only when we trust ourselves and those around us that we can lift our eyes and move toward the realization of our highest values and aspirations. The ethos grounds and connects, while the vision elevates and inspires.

This distinctively moral aspect of life is possible only in the sphere of those who trust each other and the world. This should be understood in two senses. First, trust should be taken to be a reliance on a loving gaze which includes attention and care, empathy and kindness. Second, trust is the other side of faith, which is why we often have a hard time distinguishing between them. They are intimately connected, but trust deals with how we walk on the firm ground underneath, while faith is oriented toward what is above, invisible yet present enough to guide us on our journey.

Trust and faith correlate with realism and idealism, and complement each other. To attend to something is to seek to understand what and how it truly is. In the case of human beings, it is true that we are motivated sometimes not only by empathy and kindness but also by selfishness and shallow concerns. But awareness of this should not divert our attention from the fact that there is also something good in each of us, and that the good within us, when exercised and encouraged, can grow.

Hartmann warns us to distinguish between mere credulity and wishful thinking on the one hand, versus trust and faith on the other. Additionally, trust and faith must develop over time until they become our dominant attitude toward life. Trust and faith, in a morally developed personality, will not be overridden by the disappointments and misfortunes of life. As long as we are capable of holding fast to what is good in human beings, trust and faith can lift us beyond the here and now toward great spiritual heights where we are able to discern what is ideal in humanity. In Hartmann's words, "Distant goals and vast enterprises require a different kind of faith, a faith which temporal unattainability does not stifle. It inheres in the essence of all such outlooks upon life—and these are those which lend their highest meaning to our existence—that the non-actuality of the goal does not prejudice the reality of the undertaking. Herein the potent moral element of 'not seeing and yet believing' attains its culminating point."

Prior eras in the history of human civilization have typically been dominated by either realism or idealism. In our age, however, we have turned our backs on both. When past ideals are accepted at all, they tend to appear hollow, lacking in a vibrant spirituality. And often, these ideals are openly mocked and treated as superstitions of the past eras. In place of ideals and faith, we live with anxiety and disorientation. And, unless we count our obsession with money and material goods as "realistic," we have no faith in realism either. We have grown so disoriented, we behave as if we need to defend ourselves against a random and meaningless reality, by escaping into a virtual reality.

We find ourselves in an unenviable predicament: we have little trust and even less faith. We have neither realism nor idealism; we make little effort to see human beings as they are, or to recognize the good in them, however nontransparent it may be, and however much in need of further nourishment. And yet each of us still possesses a stubborn yearning for a better world and a meaningful life. Despite our predicament, we feel an enduring longing for a vision and an ethos that can inspire confidence and encourage us to keep dreaming and fighting for what we believe in. The vision that both Kant and Hartmann endorse, which I call *the ethic of the upward gaze*, and the path of trust and faith that Hartmann suggests, offer hope that our longings are not only important to preserve but also possible to fulfill.

# 1. Pure Reason and Metaphors:
# A Reflection on Kant's Philosophy[1]

*Kant insists that we cannot learn philosophy, but we can and should learn how to philosophize. And all great philosophers use metaphors, alongside their arguments and sophisticated theories, to stimulate our philosophical thinking. Metaphors are not just figures of speech but figures of thought; they belong among the most profound expressions of a philosopher's vision insofar as they help us understand how we can, and perhaps should, look at the world, and seek our place and role in it. This essay presents and critically discusses four of Kant's central metaphors: the Copernican revolution; the island of truth and the stormy ocean of illusion; the starry heavens and the moral law; and the vision of perpetual peace. The central characteristic of Kant's metaphors is that they are about boundaries and thresholds: they present lines that divide but also mediate between different aspects and planes of existence. Their role is not only to reveal the edge of the known, but also to create a bridge toward the unknown.*

Great philosophers are often remembered more for their central metaphors than for their sophisticated doctrines. Plato's name is frequently associated with the allegory of the cave, which is familiar even to those who have never read a single line of his magnificent dialogues. Hegel's name may evoke his pronouncement of "the end of history," or the beautiful image of the owl of wisdom, Minerva, who spreads her wings at dusk, when the face of the world has already grown old. Nietzsche may be best known for his call for the re-evaluation of all values, or his image of the pitiless superman.

1    Originally published as "Pure Reason and Metaphors: A Reflection on the Significance of Kant's Philosophy," in *Annales Philosophici*, 2:2011, pp. 9–19.

Wittgenstein's name probably calls to mind the phrase "language games," or perhaps the perplexing conclusion of his *Tractatus Logico-Philosophicus*; there he first claims that "we must ... throw away the ladder after having climbed up on it," then concludes his book with the memorable statement: "Of what we cannot speak we must be silent."

Such metaphors are remembered not only for their rhetorical beauty, but because they compress intricate philosophical doctrines of great thinkers, their visions of the big picture, into a few vibrant images and captivating phrases. They find their place in our collective memory not only because of what they claim or imply, but, perhaps more importantly, because they re-orient and re-shape how we view the world and our own place and role in it. Metaphors are not simply external ornaments or effective summaries; as well as being figures of speech, they are also figures of thought. Metaphors, then, belong to the very foundation of thinking and may even be the motivation for philosophers to develop and articulate their thoughts in a systematic way.

## I. Kant's Central Metaphors

Immanuel Kant was one of greatest philosophical minds of all times, and it is helpful to recall the central metaphors that gave expression to his main concerns and convictions. His central philosophical preoccupation was with the nature and limits of "pure reason." Although always trying to develop rational thinking to its utmost boundaries, Kant did not shy away from using figurative representations. What is more, he probably believed that the use of metaphors could help us better grasp the true nature and limits of pure reason. The four such metaphors that made the strongest impression on his contemporaries and successors are: the Copernican revolution; the island of truth and the stormy ocean of illusion; the starry heavens and the moral law; and the vision of perpetual peace.

### The First Metaphor

The first of these four metaphors, Kant's Copernican Revolution, is announced in the Preface to the second edition of the *Critique of Pure Reason*: "Hitherto it has been assumed that all our knowledge must conform to objects. But all attempts to extend our knowledge of objects by establishing

7

something in regard to them *a priori*, by means of concepts, have, on this assumption, ended in failure. We must therefore make trial whether we may not have more success in the tasks of metaphysics, if we suppose that objects must conform to our knowledge."

This approach to metaphysics is very different from that signified by the Hegelian metaphor of the "owl of Minerva," whose main task is to reflect on and understand what has already happened. For Kant, as for Plato, the central task of philosophy is not descriptive and reflective but normative and transformative. Yet Kant's conception of philosophy is even more radical than that of Plato. Reason is not just a mirror of the world, nor a lamp by the light of which we can distinguish true beings from shadows and images. In yet another of his vivid metaphors, Kant compares reason to an appointed judge and lawgiver, determined to bend this world into something better than it had been heretofore. Kant's Copernican turn presents the most powerful expression of the change in the basic paradigm that was initiated by Descartes and carried out through modernity: it is not the subject who must direct himself toward the object, but the other way around. Kant's famous declaration that "we can know *a priori* of things only what we ourselves put into them" finds its full development in the Transcendental Aesthetics, where space and time are explained as *a priori* forms of intuition, and in the Transcendental Analytic, where Kant systematically arranges his categories as the basic *a priori* concepts of understanding. All experience of which human beings are capable, according to Kant, is made possible through such *a priori* elements.

### The Second Metaphor

Kant never tires of emphasizing the active and creative powers of man, but also never forgets to point out their limitations. His "creative man" is nowhere near Nietzsche's *Übermensch* (superman), and is also far more limited in creative abilities than Schiller, Fichte, Hegel, and Schelling were inclined to believe. In contrast to these German idealists, whom he inspires, but who fail to acknowledge that man's creativity is exercised in a world man does not create, Kant uses the beautiful image of a "land of truth." This land is described as an island "surrounded by a vast and stormy ocean, the native home of illusion, where many a fog-bank and many a swiftly melting iceberg give the deceptive appearance of farther shores, deluding the adventurous seafarer ever anew with empty hopes, and engaging him in enterprises which he can never abandon and yet is unable to carry to completion."

This land of truth is humanity's realm, the realm in which humans are creators and legislators; yet it is nothing more than a knowable island in the ocean of an unknowable universe. Unlike Wittgenstein, who declares a metaphysical moratorium on speech at the very end of the *Tractatus* ("Of what we cannot speak we must be silent"), Kant is convinced that it is of utmost importance to talk about and critically examine why we can never know those metaphysical issues to which we are irresistibly drawn. These questions express the deepest concerns of pure reason, and for their sake a critique of pure reason needed to be written. He holds that these concerns are ultimately reducible to three: the immortality of the soul, the existence of God, and the possibility of freedom in a mechanically determined world. Examining these issues helps us avoid deceptions regarding who we are and what we can achieve. Kant's Transcendental Dialectic shows us, for instance, that we can neither prove nor disprove the existence of God. It also leads us to recognize what Kant called "the most fortunate discovery" of pure reason: the existence of the antinomies of reason. The antinomies are the seemingly contradictory assertions—four theses and four antitheses—which claim equally strong support for themselves and reveal the permanent boundaries of human reason.

Arriving at this point of impasse, via pure reason, leads Kant to several fundamental realizations. Although Kant always gladly follows Aristotle in emphasizing that we are rational beings, the antinomical deadlock allows Kant to free himself—at least partially—from the limiting intellectualism which dominates the history of philosophy since the time of the Greeks. It also enables him to resolve the unbearable tension between science and religion, by finding it necessary to deny knowledge, in order to make room for faith. Kant's great insight is that some fundamental claims of reason cannot be decided based on evidence or reasoning alone, but must nevertheless be resolved. They can be resolved following the "needs and interests of reason," which leads Kant to substitute the foundations of intellectualism for moralism, and to argue for "the primacy of practical over theoretical reason."

## The Third Metaphor

Kant elaborates on what this primacy entails, in both the *Groundwork of the Metaphysics of Morals* and in the *Critique of Practical Reason*. In the conclusion of the latter work he states: "Two things fill the mind with ever new and increasing wonder and awe, the oftener and the more steadily we reflect on them: the starry heavens above me and the moral law within me ... The former view of a countless multitude of worlds annihilates, as it were, my importance as an animal creature, which must give back to the planet (a mere speck in the universe) the matter from which it came, the matter which is for a little time provided with vital force, we know not how. The latter, on the contrary, infinitely raises my worth as that of an intelligence by my personality, in which the moral law reveals a life independent of all animality and even of the whole world of sense—at least so far as it may be inferred from the final destination assigned to my existence by this law, a destination which is not restricted to the conditions and boundaries of life but reaches into the infinite."

Kant's friends were so impressed by this metaphor that they had the words "the starry heavens above me, the moral law within me" inscribed on his gravestone. The epitaph emphasizes the respective focal points of his thought: on one hand the cosmos, toward which his youthful passion is directed, and on the other, the moral law, the object of the almost mystical enthusiasm of his old age. In marked contrast to Plato's attitude as depicted in the cave allegory, Kant holds that the proper attitude toward these two worlds is not that of "either-or." Unlike Plato before him, or Hegel after him, Kant maintains that we are citizens of two worlds—worlds that partially overlap yet cannot be reduced to one. Just as we cannot simply choose one of the antinomical pairs and then abandon the other, we cannot avoid participation in both worlds; both are genuine, both reveal authentic aspects of our complex and divided nature. But this irrevocable dualism does not make it easier to find our proper place and role in reality. If anything, it makes finding our proper place more difficult. The phenomenal world that we can know seems to annihilate our importance as moral and spiritual beings; the noumenal world, toward which we strive and which dignifies our existence, we cannot rationally apprehend. Even if we are ignorant of it, however, this does not mean we should be indifferent toward that transcendent world. Our proper attitude toward it is that of faith.

## The Fourth Metaphor

Kant believes that such a leap of faith need not be fully irrational and tries to convince us—not always very persuasively—of the possibility of "rational faith." As to the question of the proper object of that faith, he offers several different answers. In his moral writings, it is the commensurability of virtue and happiness, under the conception of the highest good. In his writings on the philosophy of religion, it is the hope of the realization of the Kingdom of God on earth. In his historical and political writings, the focus is the vision of perpetual peace, as expressed in his famous essay "Toward Perpetual Peace: A Philosophical Sketch."

By no means a naïve or utopian thinker who would believe in an inevitable progress of humankind, Kant warns us that the phrase "perpetual peace" was inscribed over the entrance of an inn, together with a picture of a graveyard. While a graveyard may be a more romantic image of perpetual peace than a nuclear wasteland, both images portray essentially the same "solution" to the tensions burdening our world. We can hope that this is not our only path, and that the archetypal ideal of eternal peace can still be viewed in a positive manner, and help inspire a radical transformation of our desperate world.

Is it possible for us to hope for perpetual peace? In order to understand this aspiration as more than an empty wish, we must recognize that, for Kant, hope is a belief in something that is reasonably possible; it is distinct from an empty wish in that it is at least legitimate. In this spirit, Kant clarifies that the question: "What may I hope?" should be understood in connection with: "What ought I to do?" So we should approach our hope for perpetual peace in the following way: "If we do what we ought to do, can we hope for perpetual peace?"

Kant's hope is that our rational ability and moral conscience will be strong enough to steer us away from the abyss of self-destruction, away from the "idyllic" peace of the graveyard and direct us toward the creation of a much better and more just world. His thoughts about how we could become worthy of such an ideal are expressed in yet another memorable metaphor: the world can become a place in which human beings can live dignified and peaceful lives only if politics bends its knee before morality.

## II. Critical Remarks

Reflecting on the history of philosophy: Kant, if he had encountered Wittgenstein's view that we should throw away the ladder of reason after we have climbed it, would emphatically disagree. Even when insisting on "leading metaphysics to a secure path of science," he has no illusion that philosophy could ever become a closed body of knowledge, or that we should approach any philosopher with an expectation that their theories comprise the definitive pronouncements of truth. Just as there is no end of history, there is no end of philosophy. Kant holds this view both as a philosopher and as a teacher of philosophy. In the *Announcement of the Program of his Lecture for the Winter Semester of 1765–66*, he warns any student who naively thinks that "he is going to learn philosophy" that "this is impossible, for he ought to learn how to philosophize." In our own learning how to philosophize, Kant advises us to take the following words seriously: "The philosophical writer … upon whom one bases one's instruction is not to be regarded as the paradigm of judgment. He ought rather to be taken as the occasion for forming one's own judgment about him, and even, indeed, for passing judgment against him."

If we are to form our own judgment about Kant's philosophy, there is much to praise, yet also a great deal to criticize here. I will divide my criticisms into two parts, the first dealing with Kant's theoretical and the second with his practical philosophy.

Consider again Kant's famous Copernican turn. A careful analysis of the difference between the old approach, focused on ontology, and Kant's new approach, centered on epistemology, reveals something Kant himself perhaps overlooks: that his Copernican turn consists not of one but of two steps. The first step minimizes or even denies the ontological priority of the object over the subject, of being over thinking. The second step establishes a new paradigm by affirming the epistemological priority of the subject over the object, of consciousness and reason over being. We are accustomed to taking both steps together, without pausing to see whether the first needs to be followed by the second. A closer look shows that the first step does not necessarily lead to the second, as it allows for the possibility of an interactive cooperation between subject and object.

Thus, in developing his Copernican turn, Kant fails to note that, there are not just two possible model-relations between the object and the subject.

There are three. The first, which his turn abandons, is the one in which the object is treated as independent of and superior to the subject. Kant reverses this pattern, but without seeing that their relation need not be one of subordination. It could, instead, be one of cooperation. When Kant formulates the basic law of all synthetic cognition, that "the conditions of the possibility of experience in general are likewise [the] conditions of the possibility of the objects of experience," he does not realize that this agreement does not necessarily imply either transcendental subjectivism, or transcendental idealism. All that this law presupposes is that the principles of cognizing subject and the principles of the cognized object must overlap—if not fully, then to a significant degree. They could overlap for different reasons, however, and not necessarily because either the subject or the object would impose itself on the other. The overlap of the basic principles may be due to a correlation of the principles originally present in both, or it may be created in an interactive process of cognition. Kant occasionally hints at that latter possibility—for instance, when he claims that "thoughts without content are empty, intuitions without concepts are blind." Unfortunately, he quickly turns away from exploring the idea that cognition may essentially be an interactive relation, and so misses an opportunity to develop a new interactive metaphysical approach.

The metaphor contrasting the "land of truth" with the "ocean of illusion" indicates why philosophical movements such as empiricism, positivism, and pragmatism are both right and wrong. They are right insofar as they limit us to the only land we can justifiably claim as our own, the land we can control and manipulate to suit our purposes. But they are wrong insofar as they assume that the stormy ocean should cease to stir our imagination and lead us away from the familiar shore. Our needs are neither exhausted nor fully satisfied by what we can measure, control, or possess. Whatever Kant may say, metaphysics, though it may never recover its ancient status as queen of all sciences, is not going to cease to attract us.

Let us turn now to Kant's practical philosophy. He argues that our attraction to metaphysics should not cease, especially if metaphysics is understood as pertaining to the domain of morals. But here the metaphorical medium presents itself very differently. In the case of his vision of perpetual peace, the metaphor is—at least on the surface—temporal rather than spatial. Although expressed in the language of political conflicts, Kant's warning about a politics that must bend its knee before morality carries another message as well. Highly impractical and almost impossibly demanding—like the Judeo-Christian vision that inspired it—his vision is, essentially, the expectation of an inner, not an outer change; of an individual, not a social transformation. The vision of perpetual peace is an extension of Kant's most deeply rooted conviction that the ultimate test of our humanity and dignity is moral rather than political. He would agree with Aristotle that man is both a rational and a political animal. But, above all, he is a moral agent.

Our journey need not be toward some far-away ocean or distant planetary system in the starry heavens; it should be, rather, a journey toward the hidden depths of our souls, for the moral law echoes, not from the high sky above us, but from within. It is appropriate indeed that the words inscribed on Kant's grave should remind us of the starry heavens and the moral law, for this is Kant's best metaphor. It is also his worst. It is his best metaphor, for it so succinctly captures the fundamental conviction behind his multifaceted and revolutionary philosophy. But this metaphor also reveals some of his worst biases and misconceptions. Kant's vision of the complex and internally divided human nature is, ironically, neither complex nor divided enough. As our experience of art and religion reminds us, we are members of many more worlds than just the phenomenal and the noumenal. Yet, everything that may transcend the mechanical laws of nature and the moral law of the rational agent is denied neutrality, and forced into the realm of one of these two laws. Despite Kant's arguments, beauty has an independent significance of its own and cannot be reduced to "a symbol of morality," as he tries to do in the *Critique of Judgment*. Nor can religion be neatly reduced to an understanding of duties "as divine commands," as he proposes in his *Religion within the Limits of Reason Alone*.

Kant, like many other Western philosophers, seems to believe that our approach to any kind of problem or issue requires a choice between either monism or dualism. Kant clearly always opts for the latter. Reconsidering the whole issue would have been more faithful to the variety and richness of human experience, however. Kant should have questioned his own dualistic approach and tried to embrace a genuine pluralism, especially regarding values and other moral issues. Yet he does not. In moral writings, he insists on dualism: either heteronomy or autonomy, either inclinations or duties—as if no interdependence of the internal and external values and elements were possible.

Moreover, Kant overestimates the autonomous power of a rational moral agent, when he reverses the relation of volition (*Wollen*) and the moral ought (*Sollen*). As in his Copernican turn, in which the subject imposes his own *a priori* cognitive principles on the object, in his metaphysics of morals the moral law must be peculiar to the will itself, the expression of its true innermost tendency. The practical reason must prescribe its own law; the essence of good will lies precisely in this legislation. The problem is that this distorts the relation of volition to the moral ought. The ought does not determine volition; rather, volition determines the ought. While Kant's position is problematic even when taken by itself, it becomes even more so when we have to explain not only the problem of evil, but any free choice that deviates from the moral law: How is it conceivable that the will should first give the law and then transgress it?

Ethics, within philosophical theory, often treats moral problems as essentially intellectual problems, as philosophical questions in need of philosophical answers. But this is not the case. Ethical problems and ethical norms do not have any privileged status, intellectual or otherwise. They are but a fragment of a broader constellation of problems concerning the art of living. If, as Kant argues, truth is related to rationality as such, and not only to knowledge and theory, and if a way of living can be rational and irrational, then it can also be true and false. Kant should have argued not for the primacy of practical reason over theoretical reason, but for the primacy of the practical realm over the theoretical realm. The most important truths, and the most compelling illusions, are not those that we think, but those that we live by.

Many of these illusions deal with the precise nature and function of moral norms. Despite Kant's insistence, ethics cannot be merely normative, for moral laws by themselves are powerless. Moral laws know nothing about living, concrete individuals, whose lives are the only battlefields of morality. Even when morality is understood in terms of our duties and responsibilities, it cannot be understood as a dyadic relationship between a fallible rational agent and an untouchable rational norm. The relationship is better understood as triangular: moral laws and norms function as the mediators between an individual on the one hand, and other individuals—and the whole of reality—on the other. Moral laws and norms provide us with a blueprint for our interactions within the unique situations in which we find ourselves; they are no more than guidelines for our orientation in reality. Like cognition, morality does not consist in action, nor in reaction, but in interaction.

Kant not only believes in the autonomous position of morality but elevates it to the highest possible pedestal. Kant's contribution to Western philosophy is unique in that he alone attempts a metaphysical reconstruction of morals that abstracts from all anthropological considerations and presents a system of principles and duties that are seen as binding not only for all humans but for all rational beings. Yet this poses the question: are there other rational beings besides us? Even if non-human rational beings exist, how can we be sure that their rationality and morality are sufficiently like our own? More importantly, are all human beings even rational? Or are we rational merely potentially and in principle? Or only when we act as rational beings? It seems more important to focus on human beings and their moral struggles, rather than speculate about possible rational beings, whose existence or non-existence does not affect our morality.

Kant's metaphysics of morals is a glorious construction, in the best spirit of the metaphysical tradition he himself criticizes. He offers a vision of what ought to be, of the highest ideal to which a rational being can aspire. Unfortunately, it turns out that not much in Kant's vision of the metaphysics of morals and the noumenal world is at all necessary or clearly realized. The most we can say about his vision is that it is of one of many ideals that could possibly be real—a product of his creative imagination, molded by his reason. And how appealing is this vision of perfect and absolutely binding duties? If we take our willingness to act in accordance with a vision as a test of validity and truthfulness, Kant's vision does not seem very appealing or viable.

Of course, Kant would have emphatically disapproved of this test, believing as he did that even if no action is ever done out of pure duty, this still does not nullify the idea of duty, which is an "idea of reason" and not derived from experience. And logically speaking, Kant is right. It is true that even if no action were ever performed out of duty, this does not alter the potential value of the conception itself. The ideal of acting from duty may be a sufficient reason for action. However, this ideal is still not necessary. Moreover, Kant is fully aware that too frequently we opt not to act according to this ideal, and even when we do, we cannot be certain that our motives are not untainted by some "heteronomous" elements.

There is a significant discrepancy between what we do and what Kant believes we ought to do. How can this discrepancy be resolved? One of Kant's own metaphors can help us here: "If a ball does not pass through a hole, should one say that the ball is too big, or that the hole too small? In this case, it is indifferent how you choose to express yourself; for you do not know which of the two is there for the sake of the other. By contrast, you will not say that the man is too tall for his clothing, but rather that the clothing is too short for the man."

Kant's rationally constructed system of the metaphysics of morals is just like that clothing. It may be perfect for an ideal rational being, but it is unsuitable for the real man.

## III. An Occasion for Further Reflection

If we are correct in taking seriously Kant's central metaphors, an important question we must ask, to evaluate of the usefulness of his thought, has to do with their effect: Are his metaphors still capable of stimulating our thinking?

However we intend to answer this question, it must be noted that all Kant's central metaphors work together and point toward an active and creative subject. We have already indicated that his subjectivist turn has to be reconsidered, not necessarily by returning to the old doctrine of the primacy of the object, but by seriously considering how the subject and the object interact in cognitive as well as non-cognitive relations, and what each may contribute toward making these interactions possible. In connection with the nature of metaphors, however, Kant's philosophical approach opens the following questions: Would he argue that metaphors are created by us, as an expression of our active and creative nature? Or would he, along the lines of his discussion of genius in the *Critique of Judgment*, claim that the subjects expressing metaphors should be regarded more as the vehicles of some force which we cannot control or understand, but that reveals the nature of reality itself? As we can ask about Plato's use of myths, so we can about Kant's use of metaphors: Are they the expression of our creativity, or of our creativity's limitations?

It should also be pointed out that Kant's central metaphors are all about boundaries and "dividing lines": between what subjects and objects contribute to cognition; between the known and the unknown; between the visible and the invisible; between what is and what ought to be. This may be the reason why Kant's initial title for the work now known as *Critique of Pure Reason* was "On the Boundaries of Sensibility and Reason."

Some of Kant's successors—some neo-Kantians, and some positivists—wanted him to stay on this side of the dividing line and eschew any further talk about things in themselves or noumena. Their motto was: "Keep the unknown out of it, stick to the known and the knowable." This certainly was not Kant's own motto. For him, a boundary, like a threshold, belongs to both sides of the divide, keeping them in relation, however different they might be. Metaphors, by their nature, are not just the signpost of boundaries. They are also the mediators between what can and cannot be known. Their role is to reveal the edge of the known, yes, but also to create a bridge—however imperfect—toward the unknown.

## 2. Kant's Ethics of the Categorical Imperative: A Goethean Critique[1]

*This essay examines Kant's moral philosophy, only this time by focusing, not on his metaphors, but on his arguments. Kant revolutionized ethical theory by developing an ethics of duty, based on his three formulations of the categorical imperative. This imperative connects Kant's ethical theory to the concepts of rationality, of means and ends, and of autonomy and heteronomy. While Kant's theory is a major improvement over all versions of utilitarianism and consequentialism, there are still several serious problems with Kant's approach. For one thing, Kant ignores our intuitions, emotions, and spontaneous reactions. Focused on the rational principles that should have universal validity, Kant also ignores all contextual considerations. As a result, he ends up with an ethical theory that is a rational construct, too distant from his initial vision of good will as the basis for our moral orientation in the world. By focusing on good will, understood in terms of care and respect, sensitivity and love, Kant would not have offered us such a rigidly formulated moral theory but, like his contemporary Goethe, he would have presented a vision of morality more suited to actual living beings.*

Immanuel Kant succeeds in combining deep philosophical insight with rare stylistic beauty in his famous passage from the *Critique of Practical Reason* that begins with the sentence: "Two things fill the mind with ever new and increasing admiration and reverence, the more often and more steadily one reflects on them: the starry heavens above me and the moral law within me." For Kant the phrase "starry heavens" does not refer to the biblical

---

1    Originally published under the same title in *Philotheos: International Journal for Philosophy and Theology*, 8:2008, pp. 259–74.

heaven, but to "an unbounded magnitude with worlds upon worlds," which "annihilates, as it were, my importance as an animal creature, which must give back to the planet (a mere speck in the universe) the matter from which it came, matter which is for a little time endowed with vital force, we know not how." The vastness of the physical universe forces upon human beings a disturbingly humbling awareness of our relative minuteness and insignificance. As humanity's knowledge of that universe reaches further and further, our cosmic stature seems to dwindle to insignificance. Is humanity anything more than that "matter which is for a little time endowed with vital force"?

One of Kant's many claims to greatness resides in the resoluteness with which he opposes that conclusion: humankind, for Kant, transcends nature and is utterly unique. Yet the human person is so diverse and multi-faceted a creature that it is far from obvious what, if anything, makes an individual so unique. Kant unambiguously points toward morality as crucial for the proper understanding of the role and place of humanity in the universe: morality "infinitely raises my worth as an intelligence by my personality."

My task in this essay will be twofold. First I need to explain how Kant understands morality and the moral law, which he believes elevates humanity above the mechanical causality and animality of the sensible world. We will then put ourselves in a position to discuss the possibility of a genuine reconciliation of the starry heavens with the moral law. What connects them are, of course, human beings. But the question that is never fully settled in Kant's moral philosophy is: How is that reconciliation possible? How can human beings inhabit both the natural and the moral world? In Kant's view, one world is populated by the human animal, with all the powerful needs, drives, and inclinations of our bestial substratum. The other is occupied by intelligent persons possessed of free will and thereby endowed with an opportunity to strive toward the world beyond the mere here and now, to reach toward the kingdom of perfect rationality. But even if the moral law points toward a distant and more perfect world, its application must take place amid the physical world's imperfections. What, then, is the central point of morality? Is it to keep these worlds distant and to cultivate one at the expense of the other? Or is the point of morality to bring together these two worlds, and thereby the two aspects of humanity, into one world—as good as it is humanly possible to be?

# I. The Good Will

Two ideas dominate our moral experience and serve as foundational concepts for our moral theories: the concept of the good and that of the right. Although frequently used interchangeably, each of these concepts is distinct from the other, and belongs within its own framework. The good belongs to the "goal-seeking" framework, and the right to the "legalistic" or "juridical" framework. The good is related to human goals and purposes, and is understood in terms of our intentions and aspirations. The right is related to duties and obligations, and is based on modes of social organization and regulation, involving practices, rules, and laws. The good deals with values and evaluations, the right with norms and prescriptions. To value something and judge it as good does not in and of itself tell us what we ought to do. "Good" does not logically imply "right," just as "valuable" does not imply "obligatory." Nor is it the other way around. Although closely related, the good and the right are two distinct ideas.

Kant's moral philosophy is founded on a legalistic framework. His central moral concepts are those of duty, the categorical imperative, and the moral law, which are all closely related to the concept of the right. Interestingly, however, Kant begins his first and most influential work in moral philosophy, *Groundwork of the Metaphysics of Morals*, with the idea of a "good will," which suggests the good more than it does the right.

Typically, we think of a person of good will as someone who is genuinely concerned about the well-being of others, and who has a keen desire to abolish the suffering around them and make the lot of their neighbor more tolerable than it might be without their helping hand. A good will, as we envision it, manifests itself in one's direct and spontaneous sympathy for another human being; it is not based on the exchange values dictated by the market, nor is it rigidly defined by any system of duties or obligations. A good will is directed toward the future, toward what could be—toward turning the world into a better place.

This, however, is not how Kant understands a good will. A good will, in his philosophy, has nothing to do with ends and consequences, nor with natural benevolence, which Kant dismisses (by putting it in the category of "inclination") as something unstable und unpredictable, idiosyncratic and irrational. A good will, in his sense, must be universal and rational, and thus stable and predictable; it is concerned not with the future, nor with what could be, but with the timeless and unconditional "ought." This metaphysical variation on a good will is not concerned with making this world a better place, but is concerned, primarily and essentially, with itself. Kant's version of a good will is closed within itself and restricted to itself. It is, ultimately, the will that wills itself.

This Kantian "good will" is far closer to the idea of the right than to the idea of the good. Thus, it should not be surprising that Kant connects it with the concept of duty, and later, in the second section of the *Groundwork*, with his famous idea of the categorical imperative. A critical reader will quickly recognize the glaring discrepancy between our normal understanding of the good will, and Kant's categorical imperative, and that the transition from one to the other is not nearly as smooth as Kant would like us to believe. Whether Kant ever provides a successful argument that could bridge that gap is itself uncertain. The transition he proposes in section I of the *Groundwork*—based on a dubious teleology of nature and an impoverished conception of happiness—is certainly unpersuasive. Kant argues there that if nature intended us to pursue happiness as our main goal, nature would not have endowed us with the capacity of reason, for instincts, in his view, would have been more suited for this purpose. Perhaps having Goethe's *Sorrows of the Young Werther* in mind—the only work of Goethe's with which Kant was familiar—Kant then argues that a cultivated reason does not lead to happiness but rather brings more trouble upon us. The people who are more likely to be happy, according to Kant, are the simple-minded and uneducated. While happiness can, indeed, be conceived in a simple-minded fashion, as Jeremy Bentham treats it, it can be also understood in a far more sophisticated and deeper way, as in the philosophies of Plato or Aristotle. It is possible to conceive of a form of happiness that relies, not on instincts, but on the complete development and exercise of the highest human capacities, including rationality.

The problems do not stop there. It is not clear, for instance, how Kant can rely on the same teleology of nature that his own *Critique of Pure Reason* and *Critique of Judgment* revealed to be metaphysically dubious and rationally unsustainable. A nature with purposes and intentions is not the nature of the first *Critique* (nature as a starry heavens), nor could that nature rely on any objective teleology, since the third *Critique* prohibits it. Kant claims that "as nature has everywhere distributed the capacities suitable to the functions they have to perform, reason's proper function must be to produce a good will in itself and not one good merely as a means, since for the former reason is absolutely essential." Kant's line of thinking here leads to more questions than answers. What could possibly justify the claim that reason must have one, and only one, "proper function"? And why "must" that function be to "produce a good will in itself"? How does reason "produce" a good will, and what can assure us that such a will is not itself a mere rational and metaphysical construction?

To understand Kant's reasons for his emphasis on the will good in his ethical theories, we need to consider how he envisions the role of that will; to do this, we must discuss Kant's account of the categorical imperative, in which the will that is good in itself finds its expression.

## II. The Categorical Imperative

An imperative is generally understood as a command or an order of some kind. When the command or order is to perform a certain action for the sake of accomplishing a desired end, this is a hypothetical imperative. A categorical imperative, by contrast, is a command to perform an action that is objectively necessary in and of itself, without reference to some outside purpose or goal. In ordinary language we can say that a categorical imperative commands that we do something simply because it is right. For instance, we understand that if something is our duty, we have to do it, for no reason other than that it is our duty—that is, because it is the right thing to do. And in such a case we understand that it is important to act not only in accordance with duty, but out of our strong sense of duty.

Kant maintains that the categorical imperative is an unconditional imperative which "has to do not with the matter of the action and what is to result from it, but with the form and the principle from which the action itself follows." The imperative, thus understood, Kant calls "the imperative of morality" and "the moral law." Moreover, he insists that there is "one single categorical imperative" and formulates it as follows: "act only in accordance with that maxim through which you can at the same time will that it become a universal law."

As numerous critics have maintained, this formulation of the categorical imperative is not only formal, but too formal, It is also quite empty, to the point that it is not even clear how it has to do with morality, specifically. Kant's formulation of the imperative does not separate moral from non-moral actions, nor does it provide any hint of what would constitute an action's moral value.

The second formulation of the categorical imperative, by contrast, is more directly related to moral concerns: "Act so that you use humanity, in your person as well as in that of another, always as an end and never only as a means." Although this formula has the disadvantage of regulating only those actions that are related to other human beings, while disregarding those acts dealing with animals, the environment, and other morally relevant aspects of reality, at least it brings some content to the categorical imperative. Implicit in this formula is the assumption that "the human being and in general every rational being exists as an end in itself, not merely as a means to be used by this or that will at its discretion." This assumption is indicative of both the strengths and the weaknesses of the second formulation of the categorical imperative. The universalizability which is a condition for morality in the initial formulation of the categorical imperative is not a purely logical device, not a mere logical calculation. It is based, rather, on a first-person commitment to respect every other rational being as an end in itself, and an equal moral partner. This means that as a moral agent I am required to consider my universalizable maxim not only from my own idiosyncratic viewpoint, but from the perspective of every other possible moral agent. I am commanded, then, to consider my maxims from the perspective of those who are, or may be, influenced by my actions, to make sure that I am not treating them as a mere means to an end. Despite Kant's insistence that all his formulations of the categorical imperative are equivalent; the second formulation seems more fundamental than the first.

Still, this formulation of the categorical imperative has problems too. One obvious difficulty is that Kant seemingly shifts away, here, from the framework of the right and toward the framework of the good. The second formulation of the categorical imperative uses the language of "means" and "ends," which is characteristic of the goal-seeking framework. Treating humanity as an end is not directly based on any duty or obligation, but on the *worth* of humanity; and worth has to do primarily with the good, not with the right. An obligation or duty to treat humanity as an end rather than a means is secondary to and dependent on the value or worth of humanity. But this means that if that value or worth is denied or turns out to be different from what Kant affirms it to be, the obligation to treat humanity as an end would disappear.

A further problem arises from Kant's insistence on basing humanity's moral worth on our power of rationality. Whether rationality is the only human faculty Kant recognizes in his moral theory is a matter of debate, but it is unquestionable that the pillars of his moral edifice are founded on a belief in human rationality; if these pillars collapse, so will Kant's entire moral structure. If it turns out that we are mere natural beings, just grains of dust in the infinite expanse of space and time, then, within Kant's ethic, we are not ends in ourselves, and are not imbued with any kind of absolute worth. If the starry heaven is the only world humanity inhabits, Kant would have to concede that humanity is nothing more than "matter which is for a little time endowed with vital force." For morality, in Kant's worldview, to raise the worth of humanity infinitely, the human person must belong to another world: not natural but rational; not phenomenal but noumenal.

While human rationality does stand out as something unusual and unique in the natural world, this is also true of human imagination, artistic ability, language, capacity for love, and other specifically human gifts and talents. Moreover, our rationality could be seen as a curse as well as a blessing: we can calculate and represent, but also miscalculate and misrepresent; we can inform and tell the truth, but also deceive and tell a lie. Our rationality allows us to do good things, but also to do horrible things. We use rationality to invent remarkable medications and procedures which cure and eliminate otherwise deadly diseases, but we use it, also, to construct weapons far deadlier than any disease. Kant certainly knows—if on no other ground than on his own experience—how weak and unreliable an instrument the human intellect is. Why, then, does he single out rationality as the condition of an alleged absolute worth?

It would be easy to dismiss Kant's insistence on rationality as an obsessive superstition of the Enlightenment. Even though Kant is a child of the Enlightenment, however, his greatness is due in part to his being more than just a representative thinker of his era. What Kant has in common with other philosophers of the Enlightenment is his unwavering commitment to rationality and his firm faith in the power of reason. What separates Kant from them is not only his recognition of reason's insurmountable boundaries, but also his view that reason can be more than instrumental—that it can be normative. The real basis for Kant's claim that humanity must be treated as an end in itself becomes clear only when we look at his third formulation of the categorical imperative and its insistence on autonomy. As Kant explains, "the practical necessity of acting in accordance with this principle, that is, duty, does not rest at all on feeling, impulses, and inclinations but merely on the relation of rational beings to one another, in which the will of a rational being must always be regarded as at the same time *lawgiving*."

Lawgiving, that is, acting so "that the will could regard itself as at the same time giving universal law through its maxim" is what Kant calls autonomy, and he clearly states that "autonomy is therefore the ground of the dignity of human nature and of every rational nature." Our autonomy, or our legislative capacity, is what impresses Kant most about human rationality. Because of it, he regards our capacity for morality as infinitely raising our worth, and places the moral law beside (if not higher than) the stature of the starry heavens. What, then, is this capacity for lawgiving, and why would it be so important?

In the religious context, this idea of lawgiving reminds us of Moses coming down from the mountain and bringing God's "categorical imperatives" to his people. In Kant's less religiously oriented morality, every human being has the capacity to be like Moses. Although Moses "negotiates" with God, he is ultimately only a chosen messenger. Each one of us is also capable of bringing down the categorical imperative from the noumenal heights. What is more, in Kant's view each of us has the authority, which Moses does not possess, of authorizing the unconditional and absolute validity of the moral law. This is what prompts Kant to compare the moral law with the starry heavens and to assert the infinite worth of every human being.

In the *Critique of Judgment* Kant presents another line of reasoning that explains his comparison of the moral law to the starry heaven. Here, his emphasis is not on our legislative capacity and autonomy, but on our mere capacity for *respect* for the moral law, a respect which is both humbling, and related to the experience of the sublime. Kant's discussion of the sublime, although fascinating and very rich, (especially when he delves into its relation to our moral vocation and the idea of the supersensible) is among the least developed in Kant's entire opus. Nevertheless, as Lewis White Beck correctly emphasizes, "The sublimity of the moral law is more than a metaphor for Kant. Not only does he use the language of the aesthetics of the sublime in describing the moral law, but he gives an analogous interpretation of the origin of the feeling of sublimity and respect."

The language of sublimity, and of respect for the moral law, suggests that, while Kant's moral philosophy is intended to be more secular than its biblical counterpart, it should not be confused with the "completely" secular morality of the social contract. We are not merely making a voluntary and calculated agreement, or a contract, that would bind us and all other (potential or actual) members of the kingdom of rational beings. Kant's claim is more daring: we can authorize a maxim which is binding for every human being unconditionally and universally; our maxims should serve as the law for all human beings regardless of age, gender, social status, culture, nationality, or religious affiliation. They are binding as the law regardless of our material, psychological, or spiritual situations. As a legislator, I must ignore all the specific conditions and restrictions of my existence. My maxims should serve as the law for myself and any human being living now, or in the future, or even in the past. This is what elevates us above Moses and brings us closer to God than Moses ever was.

## III. Criticism of Kant's Moral Theory

Certainly, Kant's view of our legislative ability is open to objections. Perhaps the most common objection is that what he demands of us is impossible. For one thing, we do not exercise our rational capacity in the way that Kant suggests; humans are not the legislators that Kant expects them to be. One main reasons for this is that our rationality is not as uniform and unchanging as Kant assumes. For us, the word "reason" has long since lost its unequivocal simplicity. We no longer believe in the unity and immutability of reason. Thus, even if we attempt to be such universal legislators, it is unlikely that we would all universalize our maxims in the same way, or all agree about the absolute worth of humanity.

Moreover, history challenges Kant's metaphysics of morals in general, and his view of our legislative capacity in particular. History, especially twentieth-century history, has cast a vast shadow of doubt over our past optimism about the unquestionable moral progress of the human species. Insofar as we are willing to associate any kind of good will with humanity, we must also be prepared to account for the unspeakable evils that are committed by humanity and in the name of humanity. If morality is what separates us from the natural world, it makes us unique not only in the positive but in the negative sense. If morality is what makes us God-like, it also makes us diabolical.

As serious as these objections are, they do not get to the heart of what is most problematic in Kant's moral philosophy. Set aside, for the moment, the fact that we rarely, if ever, exercise our supposed legislative capacity in the way Kant intends, and set aside also the question of why. Set aside Kant's questionable belief in the unity and universality of reason. Yes, we are appalled by the human evil that surrounds us, but so was Kant: there was hardly a year without war and violence in his century; millions of people groaned under the yoke of servitude and tyranny; the slave trade flourished; witchcraft was still punishable by death. It is precisely for such and similar reasons that we cannot rely on what humanity has been, or is, but must focus on what humanity ought to become.

To object that it is psychologically impossible, or against our nature, to live up to Kant's standards, is to miss the point. What he envisions is an ideal that is possible for every rational human being. We all understand what Kant means when he maintains that, for instance, making a false promise is unconditionally impermissible, or that truthfulness is our absolute duty. And the fact that Kant's rigorous morality demands that we turn away from our pursuit of happiness to follow the call of duty does not necessarily speak against him. To be sure, it may be difficult for us to live up to Kant's standard. But difficult does not mean impossible. Kant may be quite right to demand a genuine transformation of our moral attitudes: if the world is to become a better place, something radical may be needed to wake us from our moral slumber. The most important question still remains: Is Kant's morality of the categorical imperative, together with his view of what constitutes the dignity of humanity, the only way, or even the best way, to bring about that transformation?

I answer that it is neither. To justify this criticism, let us first make a necessary detour.

Human thought has two basic options for accounting for reality: one is based on an idea of creation, while the other accounts for reality in organic (or biological) terms. The former attempts to account for the beginning (and frequently the end) of the world in relation to a creator (e.g., God), or at least in terms of an act of creation (e.g., the Big Bang). The latter does not assume that reality must have either a beginning or an end, and conceives of reality as an organically structured complex, perpetually changing and growing.

As these approaches can be used for a general account of reality, they can also be used to account for the phenomenon of morality. The creation model is frequently associated with laws (*nomoi*), which is what Kant is doing when he claims, for instance, that "everything in nature works in accordance with laws," and then makes the "ethical" turn: "Only a rational being has the capacity to act in accordance with the representation of laws, that is, in accordance with principles, or has a will. Since reason is required for the derivation of action from laws, the will is nothing other than practical reason."

Kant bases his metaphysics of morals on the model of creation, comparable to the one on which Christianity is founded. As the Bible proclaims that in the beginning was *logos*, so also does Kant believe that morality is based on *logos*, or, more precisely, on a *noetic* (rational) act of legislating a universally and unconditionally valid law. Considering the way Kant establishes the absolute goodness of the good will in the *Groundwork*, it may not be farfetched to claim that the *Groundwork* is structured as "The Book of the Genesis of Morality." The creator in Kant's account is not God, however, but the human individual: the legislative capacity elevates the person above the natural world and glorifies their being as an absolute end.

The use of this analogy may be the ultimate source of the difficulties with Kant's ethics of respect for the law. The analogy misleads him into a distorted reconstruction of the phenomenon of morality, and leads him to advocate for an untenable view on the role and place of humanity in the universe. While it may be acceptable, in the biblical account, for the perfect creator and the imperfect creation to be separated from each other by an unbridgeable gap, it makes little sense to envision that one and the same being, the human person, could be so irreconcilably divided as to belong to two separate worlds.

In terms of its theoretical rationally legislative capacity, humanity, in Kant's philosophy, is elevated to the highest possible rank and ascribed an absolute worth. Yet this same humanity, in the sense of living, real individuals, is utterly ignored and depreciated. Instead of a single cohesive vision of one humanity, we end up with two: one a frozen, abstract absolute and the other a forever changing and fundamentally irrelevant individual. One side has a norm: formal and flawless, but without vitality; the other has energy: potent and vibrant, but without a reliable sense of direction. Humanity, in Kant's moral philosophy, thus achieves an ambiguous and paradoxical status.

It is a mistake to tie the dignity of human beings entirely, or even primarily, to our legislative capacity and autonomy. It is also wrong to reduce all morally relevant modes of human relationships to this somewhat mechanical relation of means and ends. It is possible for one person to treat another with an utter disregard for their personality and individuality, even if they are not treating them as an instrumental means for achieving certain goals or purposes. Or we may simply treat one another as though we were all polite strangers with no interest in anyone else's affairs, problems, or aspirations. This type of non-abusive and distantly respectful relationship may serve as a blueprint for the necessary minimum for a society in which people respect one another's basic human rights, but it certainly does not serve as a model for a good, genuine, and authentic human relationship. We may value human beings, and indeed all living beings, simply because we are parts of the same whole—the whole of reality. Yet just as the means-ends relation is not a specifically and strictly moral relation, the part-whole relation is not specifically and strictly moral either. A more detailed study of specifically human relationships would have to include relationships of giving and taking, as well as relationships where one is simply present with and for another, and those where one listens to the other, cares for the other, and so forth.

We can find an excellent example of a more spontaneous and creative perspective on the morality of relationships in Kant's contemporary, Johann Wolfgang von Goethe. Like Kant, Goethe was opposed to understanding the good in terms of self-interest and utility. Furthermore, like Kant, Goethe had a developed perspective on the importance of duty. Unlike Kant, he did not associate our duties with any one single categorical imperative. When the question was posed to him, about what a person's duty might be, Goethe offered a characteristic reply: "It is what the day demands."

Goethe's reply indicates a genuine sensitivity to the morally relevant aspects of the situation in which a moral agent may find themself. Kant, unfortunately, wants to preclude precisely that, at least at the level of the categorical imperative. His good will is closed in on itself and does not reflect or relate to the complexities of context. This approach does have a positive side, insofar as Kant does not make the ideal of goodness relative to the situation. Yet Kant's self-enclosed will has a down side as well. Not only is it detached from reality; it hinges on a denial of reality, insofar as it refuses to factor in that which is, in its determination of what ought to be done.

Goethe's cryptic reply is related to another aspect of the problem of elucidating an accurate account of morality. To know what my duty is, it is not enough simply to be sensitive to the morally relevant aspects of the situation in which one finds oneself; one must also make a judgment about that situation. And making a moral judgment is a far more important, and far more difficult aspect of morality, than moral legislation is.

Kant may object that if one has not first determined the correct principle of morality, their judgment is, if not impossible, then necessarily clouded and potentially misleading. Kant compares the moral law with a compass and claims that "with this compass in hand" an ordinary man "is well able to distinguish, in all cases that present themselves, what is good or evil, right or wrong." This view, however, is both overly ambitious, and misguided; it sounds impressive in theory but is not very helpful in practice. For even without establishing *the* moral principle, most people would agree that honesty and sincerity, self-control and patience, respect and humility, gratitude and forgiveness, and diligence and thoroughness in the performance of our daily duties and tasks are of central moral significance. When we have those in mind, we are unlikely to treat others merely as means, rather than as ends in themselves. When our moral judgment is not overshadowed by excessive self-centeredness, when we are sufficiently open and sensitive toward ourselves, others, and reality, we really do not need any specific and definite moral law, nor do we need to worry much about the right formulation of the categorical imperative. The principle of morality, if there needs to be such a thing, could be formulated as Goethe put it: "Do good for the sheer love of goodness!"

If we may call Goethe's scattered reflections a moral view, this would be an example of an ethic based on an organic approach to reality. When morality is based on the organic model, it is pointless to ask whether man is the ultimate purpose of creation, an end in himself, a creature with an absolute worth, or anything similar. What matters is the whole, not any hierarchy within the whole. As far as humanity is concerned, what matters most of all is whether human beings are integrated into the whole of reality, so that this whole can persist in a harmonious way.

Unfortunately, self-centered humanity has shown little respect for the harmony of nature. This lack of respect manifests itself in both our private lives and our social world, and calls for a transformation of our moral attitudes. The question is, then: what should this transformation entail? Unlike Kant and like Goethe, I do not believe that the transformation of our moral attitude requires a strict and fixed hierarchy of laws and principles. On the contrary, it calls us to abandon such hierarchies. We intuitively understand the general structure of the network of interrelated values and duties in our world.

This being the case, the real moral challenge is not to build a metaphysics of morals, but to apply these intuitively grasped values to concrete, living situations. We don't need to establish the form of the moral law, prior to and independent of any material concern; rather, we need to be sensitive to the situation in which we find ourselves, so that we can find the correct form for channeling already existing and intuitively understood values and principles. For instance, it is obvious to every sane person that we should love our children, and that we have a duty to create for them the best possible opportunities for their development and flourishing. But this requires a thorough sensitivity to who those children are, their general and individual needs, relevant circumstances, and opportunities, and how to translate our love and our concern for them into practice. Where so much can go wrong, where so many of us fail as parents, is precisely in finding the proper ways of showing our love, encouragement, and support, and in finding the proper ways to stimulate the children's development.

As Martin Buber sums up, in a cryptic spirit reminiscent of Goethe's: "The distinction to be made here is not between norm and norm, but between way and way." The sad condition of the world is not due to our lacking a moral law, or not knowing how to legislate the proper formulation of the categorical imperative. It is not because empirical inclinations make it impossible for us to follow the call of duty. To argue this would be to misrepresent or distort the phenomenon of morality. What we need, if we are to be truly moral and make the world better, is something far simpler, as close to our hearts as it is to our minds. What we need is more sensitivity towards others, and to the world. Such a sensitivity should replace our ignorance and indifference, and compel us to interact with others more benevolently. What we need, in fact, is more good will.

If Kant is right in claiming that our moral capacity elevates us and makes us unique, this is not because of our legislative capacity but because of our ability and responsibility to make moral judgments and act in accordance with them. In judging and acting morally, we do not have contempt for or reject reality, but interact with and participate in it. If humanity can develop and blossom morally, it is in this same reality to which the starry heavens also belong. And if morality can lead to a better and more perfect world, this world has to be built not in the invisible noumenal heights, but in the midst of the imperfections of our human world. Whether a person can legislate the categorical imperative or not, they are still capable of sound judgment, benevolence, love, and genuine compassion. And that should be enough to command as much respect and admiration for human beings as we have for the starry heavens.

# 3. Respect for Persons:
# Hartmann's Reinterpretation of Kant[1]

*This essay continues with a critical examination of Kant's ethical theory, but this time by developing it further rather than by straight-forwardly criticizing his arguments. One way to approach Kant's ethics is in terms of the concepts of persons and personality, and the respect that the moral law demands we show for them. Kant's theory is open to three kinds of objections. First, the line separating and also connecting humanity and personality is not clearly delineated. Second, person and personality are reconstructed in terms of being rational moral agents, but without taking into account any individual uniqueness of those agents. Third, the respect to be shown to other persons, as commended by the moral law, is merely intellec-tual: it ignores every emotional component, without which respect remains an abstraction devoid of any positive meaning. The concept of personality needs to be expanded to become more context-sensitive and also adjusted to each individual; the ideal of universality in its relevance to action can only be developed along with the recognition of what is involved in unique individuality. The concept of respect for persons must, despite Kant, be understood in terms of the care and love which individuals have for each other.*

Having begun by critiquing Kant's ethical theory in general, I will now ex-amine his conception of person and personality in terms of respect for the moral law. While this is not the only way to understand Kant's conception, it may be the most important one. In this first part of this discussion, I will

---

1   Originally published under the same title in *Cultivating Personhood: Kant and Asian Philosophy*, ed. Stephan Palmquist (New York: Springer Verlag, 2010), pp. 485–92.

offer a brief clarification of the relevant concepts of persons and personality. In the second part, in light of some remarks by Nicolai Hartmann, I will examine the notion of respect for persons, as well as adjacent issues relevant for understanding what it means to show respect to others. This second part will raise more questions than it will offer answers. I hope these questions will lead to further considerations of Kant's rich, yet never fully developed conception of person and personality.

## I. Personality and Respect

Kant's consideration of person and personality fits into the general framework of modern philosophy, but also has its own peculiar characteristics. Following a broadly Christian tradition, Kant accepts the fundamental dualism in human nature and associates the seat of personality with the soul, not the body. Following Descartes, modern philosophy narrows its focus, shifting attention from the broad sphere of "soul" to the narrower sphere of "mind." Many modern philosophers even base their ethics on the philosophy of mind. In accordance with this modern preoccupation with the mind, in Kant's philosophy of personality can be understood in connection with his idea of the transcendental unity of apperception, with the unity of all theoretical or practical activity, or in terms of autonomy.

Iris Murdoch remarks that, in the Cartesian tradition, an agent is envisioned as a kind of isolated principle of the will. She adds that in this tradition, "the agent's freedom, indeed his moral quality, resides in his choices, and yet we are not told what prepares him for the choices."

Kant's theory of personality does not seem to suffer from this omission. In *Religion within the Limits of Reason Alone*, Kant introduces the concept of personality in the context of his discussion of our several predispositions. The term "predisposition" (*Anlage*) is Kant's way of talking about basic human nature as it is prior to any actual exercise of freedom. Kant's three "original predispositions" are those of animality, humanity, and personality. These predispositions correspond roughly to: (1) physical love that provides for the preservation of the species; (2) self-love that is both physical and rational, producing the inclination to "acquire worth in the opinion of others"; and (3) "the capacity for respect for the moral law" as a sufficient incentive for the will.

Consider now these three predispositions in terms of what deserves our proper respect. Kant does not have much admiration for animality. He believes that life as such has no intrinsic value; it has value only with regard to the use to which we put it, the ends to which we direct it.

So, what is it that deserves our respect? Is it humanity? Or should such respect be reserved only for personality?

This issue is not properly resolved in Kant's philosophy. What is clear is that, if human life is to acquire value, or be treated as valuable, this must happen at a higher level than that of animality. Yet, at least on the surface, the next level up, that of humanity, is the most controversial of the three predispositions. This is also where Kant's interpreters differ the most. While Christine Korsgaard, for instance, equates this predisposition with a capacity to set ends, Yermiyahu Yovel understands it more broadly in terms of finite rational being, which for Kant also includes the relevant "unsociable sociability." Whether understood narrowly or broadly, humanity, for Kant, is a precondition for personality, or for the state of morality. Humanity itself is not necessarily a moral state, but it is required for morality to be possible.

It seems that this possibility is sufficient to assign to human beings an absolute value—the value of dignity and autonomy. In various contexts, Kant formulates his ideas regarding the value of human beings (as moral beings) in different ways. Most of them seem to converge in one point: respect for the moral law. Personality, for Kant, is an Idea of reason, and it is not a given. We are persons, yes, but no finite sensible being can be fully adequate to the Idea of personality. In human beings, considered empirically, we find at most only a "predisposition to personality," which is the capacity for respecting the moral law enough so that it is sufficient incentive for the will.

I interpret Kant's claim that personality is an Idea of reason in the following way. Morality conceives of a world that does not yet exist in nature or society, and seeks to actualize it by acting, in the given world, according to the laws of the possible world. In Kant's words, "[the moral] law gives to the sensible world, as sensuous nature (as this concerns rational beings), the form of an intelligible world, i.e., the form of supersensuous nature, without interfering with the mechanism of the former."

The key to understanding Kant's ethics lies in the relationship between reason and will, a relationship that is marked by the distinctive feeling of respect (*Achtung*). Respect is "a positive feeling not of empirical origin ... which can be known *a priori* ... a feeling produced by an intellectual cause." Put differently, "Sensuous feeling ... is the condition of the particular feeling we call respect, but the cause that determines this feeling lies in the pure practical reason." It is evident from Kant's remarks that this respect can have no ground but a moral one. Furthermore, respect applies to persons only: "All respect for a person is properly only respect for the law ... of which the person provides an example." What is less clear is exactly how respect applies to persons: that is, how can we show such respect?

This question deals not only with the ground of respect, but with its scope, and with its negative and positive manifestations. If respect is something other persons do not have to earn, or cannot fail to earn (simply because they are rational beings and moral agents), does that mean respect for them is a moral obligation? Must other persons always be respected? Must all persons be respected? Must all persons be treated with equal respect, or is there a difference in the degree of respect due to one person versus another? Must each person, in order to be respected, be treated in the same way? How about the individual differences between persons, or their actual behavior: Are these things irrelevant? Does a rapist deserve the same respect as a morally virtuous person? Does a murderer?

Many ethicists, some of whom are Kant's followers, do not believe that the equality of all persons means that all persons must be treated the same way. Treating people with respect, these ethicists argue, does not mean treating them equally. This approach makes sense: there is no reason to view Kant's belief as being so rigid, or as providing some unchangeable, *a priori* calculus. Yet if it is possible that treating people with respect takes different forms, what accounts for the difference? And how is the difference acknowledged?

One plausible approach to this latter question is to make a distinction between the negative and the positive aspects of respect. The negative aspect of respect, should be invariable, and at the very least it should involve refraining from regarding or treating other persons in morally inappropriate ways. For example, in accordance with the second formulation of the categorical imperative, other persons should never be treated as a mere means. This should hold true, regardless of their behavior, or their motives for their behavior, because every person must be treated as an end in themself, insofar as they are a free rational being possessing dignity.

The positive aspect of respect, however, considers individual differences—not all differences, but the relevant ones. The relevant differences involve a person's actual behavior and motives. A rapist or a murderer who intentionally harms others must be treated differently—although with respect—than a morally virtuous person. A morally virtuous person is shown respect in a positive way, because such a person, as a free and rational moral agent, acts from the conception of duty; a rapist or a murderer does not. In punishing a rapist, for instance, we obviously treat such a person differently than the one who is morally virtuous. Kart argues that, nevertheless, in punishing such a person, we must also treat them with respect insofar as we assume that, as a free and rational agent, this person could (and should) have chosen to act differently.

Are there other differences we should consider as well? After all, we often associate personality with individuality. Though all humans have much in common, we all have unique individual characteristics also, and these traits are important for who we are. Can Kant's ethics take such variances into consideration? And should it?

## II. Personality and Individuality

Hartmann has pursued these questions with exceptional persistence, and has come up with some ingenious perspectives worth mentioning here. He connects Kant's views on the ethical treatment of persons, in relation to respect for the moral law, with the first formulation of the categorical imperative. Insofar as this formulation affirms that the moral test for every action is whether its maxim could be made a universal law, Hartmann points out, there is something here which, in principle, a human being, as a personality, cannot intend. This is because, to apply Kant's formulation, we would have to will, at the same time, that the maxim not only be universalizable, but each person's conduct should resemble our own. But this is something no one ought to do—or ought to need to do. This requirement would reduce human beings to mere numbers in the crowd who could be replaced by anyone. So our personal existence becomes empty and meaningless.

Hartmann believes that, based on such a concern, one could formulate a law that would run contrary to Kant's categorical imperative. This law would say something like: "So act that the maxim of thy will could never become the principle of a universal legislation without a reminder." Or: "Never act solely on the basis of a system of universal values; one must also act in accordance with the individual values of your own person."

There is clearly a discrepancy here. As Hartmann demonstrates, following Kant leads to an antinomy that cannot be fully removed. But perhaps the most surprising aspect of Hartmann's treatment of this issue is that he does not believe this antinomy creates any essential problem for Kant's account of persons and respect for the moral law. On the contrary, he believes it complements and enriches Kant's view.

Here is how Hartmann reaches this conclusion. The real demand of Kant's categorical imperative is: "I ought to will, as under literally the same circumstances everyone else ought to will." But "literally the same circumstances" would entail the unique and distinctive nature of my individual ethos. "The imperative, accordingly, when the complete structure of the case is born in mind, not only excludes the moral justification of a will exactly the same in others, but it positively demands also the unique factor in my own will, without prejudice to the classification which brings my will and that of others under a rude uniformity of the Ought. The Ought allows unlimited scope for an individually articulated will."

Hartmann concludes from this that individuality could not, and should not, be excluded from moral considerations. Nor could or should it be excluded from the proper understanding of what it means to be a person, or what it means to show respect for persons. Although this may be an unintended consequence of Kant's theory, or perhaps something simply overlooked by Kant, Hartmann concludes that "the categorical imperative has within itself its own opposite. It involves its own converse. Its limitations lie not outside it, but in it."

## III. Personality, Respect, and Love

While discussing Hartmann's revisionist reading of Kant's theory of personality and respect for persons, a few more points should be mentioned. As is well known, Kant strictly opposes acting out of pity or love. Such acting, for Kant, would effectively eliminate our respect for the persons we pity or love, as free rational agents. Emotions such as pity or love should not be a factor in our actions, because they make it impossible to treat others with the (negative) respect to which they are entitled, and which they as moral agents cannot fail to earn. Hartmann argues that Kant thereby unnecessarily restricts his own theory, and distorts both the idea of the nature of personality and the goal of respect for other persons.

Here, briefly, is what Hartmann has in mind. Kant's moral philosophy is often interpreted in terms of his opposition to "inclinations" and his focus on moral categories, such as justice. There may be good reasons for this. If, for example, we think of justice in comparison to love (e.g., brotherly love), there can be an antinomical opposition between them. In Hartmann's succinct formulation, "Justice may be unloving, brotherly love quite unjust." Following the Stoics, Kant treats love as a pathological inclination. Yet this aspect of love is not its most important characteristic, nor its ethically relevant manifestation. Love can also be understood in terms of disposition or intention. In this sense, love is not only close to what Kant calls "good will," but is also essential to our treatment of other persons and our respect for them. As Hartmann puts it, "[justice] joins person to person, but only surface with surface ... Brotherly love binds them far more deeply ... Personal love, however, unites forthwith innermost depth to innermost depth, overleaping the surfaces."

Hartmann's remarks should lead us to reconsider Kant's understanding of respect for persons. Kant, we recall, distinguishes three predispositions—of animality, of humanity, and of personality—and seems inclined to treat respect for persons in terms of the disposition of personality. This is due the ties that exist between this disposition and the moral law. As quoted earlier, Kant maintains: "All respect for a person is properly only respect for the law ... of which the person provides an example." Following Hartmann's remarks, we realize that such a conception is too narrow. If, because of its connections with the moral law, the disposition to personality is the only proper object of respect, too much is left out, even in the moral context. As Hartmann points out, love cuts deeper than justice and other values that would be regulated by the moral law.

Two options may be open, then. Option one would be to broaden, significantly, the range of respect, at least enough to include the predisposition of humanity, maybe even to include some aspects of animality. The second option is to introduce two different kinds of respect: one in a narrow moral sense, focusing on personality and the moral law, and the other broader, including the whole range of human predispositions and capacities. I am suspicious of the ground on which such a line could be drawn, however. If personality is only "an idea of Reason," staking the most important form of respect on something of that kind seems too constricted. As Murdoch pointed out, "the agent's freedom, indeed his moral quality, resides in his choices, and yet we are not told what prepares him for the choices." The moral law deals with freedom and the agent's choices. To understand what allows for such choices, Hartmann offers a plausible suggestion that we need to consider all the agent's dispositions and capacities, both rational and non-rational. Is not the entire human being, then, that which deserves our respect?

# 4. Transdisciplinarity as an Interactive Approach[1]

*During the twentieth century, we witnessed a shift toward narrow specializations in all branches of science and philosophy. At the beginning of the twenty-first century, such an approach is criticized not only for blocking fruitful cooperation between various disciplines but also because of the harmful consequences of such narrowly focused research for our overall well-being. In this essay, I critically examine and further develop Basarab Nicolescu's "transdisciplinarity" proposal: a quantum physicist by profession, Nicolescu voices justified concerns that our present intellectual efforts endanger the further prospering and even the very existence of the human race. He proposes a new integrative approach in terms of "three pillars of transdisciplinarity," recognizing that reality is complex and multi-layered and our thinking too linear to deal with that reality in an adequate way. Inspired by Hartmann, I argue that the pillars of transdisciplinarity should be interpreted slightly differently than Nicolescu suggests and that we also need a fourth pillar that would allow us to examine the nature and function of values. Perhaps only in that way can we still bring about a reversal of the self-destructive course of our civilization.*

We are witnessing, I am convinced, the first stages of a promising new movement. This movement promotes a new approach to human knowledge, ranging from and including natural sciences, social sciences, and humanities. Indeed, this is a new approach to humanity in general. The current name of this revolution is "transdisciplinarity," and one of its most

---

1   Originally published as "Transdisciplinarity as an Interactive Method: A Critical Reflection on the Three Pillars of Transdisciplinarity," in *Integral Leadership Review*, October 2009 (an online journal).

important pioneers and champions is the quantum physicist Basarab Nicolescu. As the author of *La transdisciplinarité*, the initial manifesto of the transdisciplinary movement, he continues to develop this new vision of human knowledge and a new approach to the world in which we live together. My goal here is to contribute to the development of this new paradigm by offering a sympathetic yet critical reflection on the fundamental philosophical and methodological aspects of transdisciplinarity. I will begin, in section I, by discussing the word "transdisciplinary" and arguing that transdisciplinarity should be understood as an interactive method. After that, I will consider (in sections II-IV) the so-called "three pillars of transdisciplinarity: the levels of Reality, the logic of the included middle, and complexity," which Nicolescu claims "determine the methodology of transdisciplinary research." What is initially unclear are two things: First, why are there exactly three pillars, rather than two, or four, or any other number? Second, why these particular pillars, rather than any others? After suggesting why Nicolescu's three pillars should be organized as transdisciplinary ontology, transdisciplinary logic, and transdisciplinary epistemology, I will in the end (section V) argue for the inclusion of a fourth pillar as well. Nicolescu himself often emphasizes the value aspect of transdisciplinarity; namely that it is a way of self-transformation, oriented towards the knowledge of the self, the unity of knowledge, and the creation of a new art of living. For this reason transdisciplinarity requires the fourth pillar as well, a new transdisciplinary theory of values.

## I. Transdisciplinarity and Interaction

In Nicolescu's work, the prefix "trans" indicates that "transdisciplinarity concerns that which is at once between the disciplines, across the different disciplines, and beyond all disciplines. Its goal is the understanding of the present world, of which one of the imperatives is the unity of knowledge. There are many reasons to avoid the trap of increasingly fragmented disciplinary research, and even interdisciplinary and multidisciplinary approaches do not offer fully satisfactory ways to do so. For one thing, such approaches remain fixed on a few aspects of reality and do not attempt to understand it as a whole. And a deeper problem, which is perhaps the reason for our fragmented approach, concerns our basic assumptions about the nature of

43

reality. A brief reminder about the two most frequently accepted models— one classical and one modern—can illustrate this point:

According to the first model—the ancient and scholastic view of the priority of object over subject—being and thinking are not ontological equals. Being here is treated as having its own firmly established identity and unity, independent of and indifferent to whether it is known. "To be" is to be a definite kind of thing. If our thinking is to disclose what being is, it must adjust itself to the properties of being.

According to the second model—the modern view of the epistemological prevalence of subject over object—being and thinking are not epistemological equals. Thinking has priority over being, insofar as it is more easily accessible than being. In order to be known, being must adjust to the structures of thinking. "To be" is to be an object of possible knowledge; it is to be knowable as a certain kind of thing.

Both these models share at least three assumptions that no longer seem tenable. First, both models treat reality as something static, not dynamic. Second, both models assume a complete separation of thinking from being, of subject from object. And third, both assume there must be a hierarchical relation between subject and object, between thinking and being; each model takes one as dominant over the other, without considering that they might be in a cooperative rather than competitive relation.

All of these assumptions have been justly criticized. Nicolescu often speaks about Nature, rather than reality, and—with full awareness that it is a pleonasm—emphasizes the expression "living Nature." He is right to insist that, "the study of living Nature asks for a new methodology—transdisciplinary methodology—which is different from the methodology of modern science and the methodology of the ancient science of being. It is the coevolution of the human being and of the universe which asks for a new methodology."

I am convinced that Nicolescu is right, yet instead of the fairly general expression "coevolution," it would be more precise to say "interaction," a word which he himself uses frequently. What are interactive relations? We do not have a comprehensive understanding of them, but several elementary points about them are clear.

1. Interactions are dynamic, not static, relations. Their conditions, parameters, or even objectives can change with different circumstances and over a period of time, without thereby interrupting the relations themselves.

2. Interactive relations are always reciprocal; this is what distinguishes them from one-directional relations, such as actions or reactions. This reciprocity can take many forms, depending on the elements or forces involved. We can distinguish, for instance, between interdependence, interchange, intercourse, interlinking, interfusing, interplaying, etc.

3. The positive value of interactive relations is expressed and measured not in "oppositional" or "hierarchical," terms, but in "cooperative" and "complementary" terms. This value is expressed and measured not through zero-sum hierarchies and power-relations, such as losing and winning, controlling and being controlled, manipulating or being manipulated; rather, the positive value of interactions is shown in terms of proper functioning and fitting, balance and harmony, authenticity and growth.

4. Interactions can take place between quite heterogeneous elements and forces; homogeneity is not a prerequisite for interaction. This means that in our attempts to understand reality, we can observe interactions between the inorganic and the organic, between the organic and the psychic, or between the psychic and the spiritual, without having to force every phenomenon into any of the often artificially defended monisms, whether of a materialistic kind (as in modern science), or of an idealistic kind (as in Leibniz or Hegel).

For an interactive transdisciplinary methodology, a genuine pluralistic and dynamic approach to reality is the foundation of all research and of every attempt to understand our place and role in that reality. But to see in more detail what this interactive transdisciplinary methodology amounts to, we need to take a closer look at each of the proposed pillars of transdisciplinarity.

## II. Levels of Reality and Transdisciplinary Ontology

The first, and perhaps the most fundamental, of the three pillars of transdisciplinarity is the view that reality is multi-dimensional, that it has different and mutually irreducible levels. Thinking primarily of the difference between the quantum and microphysical levels of reality, Nicolescu maintains that "two levels of Reality are different if, while passing from one to the other, there is a break in the laws and a break in fundamental concepts (such as, for example, causality)." The idea is that, regardless of the capabilities of our intelligence and the actual level of our knowledge, the very structure of reality is discontinuous, yet this discontinuity does not prevent different layers from coexisting and interacting in a variety of ways.

Nicolescu points out that "the existence of different levels of Reality has been affirmed by different traditions and civilizations, but this affirmation was founded either on religious dogma or on the exploration of the interior universe." Rigorous attempts to handle several difficult problems in quantum physics and mathematics have given a new credibility to this old view, which has always lingered in the undercurrents of Western views of reality but has—up to now—never emerged as the predominant paradigm. Nicolescu is obviously inspired by Kurt Gödel and his insight that a sufficiently rich system of axioms inevitably leads to results which would be either undecidable or contradictory. Nicolescu also singles out the contributions of Heisenberg, Pauli, and Bohr. He cites with approval Heisenberg's conception of the three regions of reality: (i) that of classical physics, (ii) that of quantum physics, biology, and psychic phenomena, and (iii) that of religious, philosophical, and artistic experience. Nicolescu himself proposes a distinction between Objective Nature, Subjective Nature, and Trans-Nature, which taken together define living Nature, and toward the examination of which the transdisciplinary approach is directed.

Mathematicians and physicists are not the only ones who offer significant contributions to our understanding of the different levels of reality; think, for instance, of the contributions by Arthur Koestler ("holons"), Ken Wilber ("Four Quadrants of the Kosmos"), and others. And if we consider ancient history, we are reminded that different approaches to and understandings of reality have always existed in Western philosophy. Nicolescu mentions Aristotle and Heraclitus in particular as representatives of two opposite approaches: on one hand the static and rational, on the other, the relational and intuitive. Transdisciplinarity certainly does not exclude rationality; nevertheless, the relational, intuitive, and interactive features play a leading role.

Multiple philosophers have similarly contributed to our understanding of the multi-dimensionality of reality. Nicolescu mentions Edmund Husserl, as well as "other scholars [who] have detected the existence of different levels of perception by the subject-observer of Reality." He correctly adds that these thinkers "were pioneers in the exploration of a multidimensional and multireferential reality." Unfortunately, "they have been marginalized by academic philosophers and misunderstood by physicists, with each area being trapped in its respective specialization."

I cite Nicolescu's reference to Husserl because I would like to call attention to the work of a philosopher who further developed Husserl's phenomenological method and whose enormous philosophical opus is centered on the idea of multilayered reality. This now unjustly neglected philosopher is Nicolai Hartmann. His revolutionary works emerged in the thirties and forties of the twentieth century, at the same time when physics was opening new frontiers of a complex multidimensional reality. Since Hartmann's insights could be of extreme importance for the further development of the transdisciplinary vision, I will outline several of his central ontological doctrines.

In the history of Western philosophy and science, thinkers have concocted various kinds of monisms and dualisms in their attempt to capture the structure of reality, but Hartmann thinks that all are based on oversimplifications and distortions; they "involve prejudice in favor of simplicity." Hartmann argues in favor of ontological pluralism; he thinks that our map of real being must be complex and multidimensional, for reality displays a multiplicity of forms that cannot be reduced to one or two ultimate principles. A phenomenological analysis clearly reveals four distinguishable and irreducible strata of reality: inorganic, organic, psychic, and spiritual. It is easy to distinguish between inanimate objects, plants, animals, and humans (as individuals and as members of society). All four strata are interconnected and can be compared in terms of their respective strength and height within their hierarchy. In terms of height, spirit is above all other strata, but cannot exist without them; the higher strata are attached to and dependent on the lower for their energies and support. In terms of strength, the following principle holds: the lower the strata, the stronger and more basic they are. The lower strata are always included in the higher ones, but not the other way around.

This phenomenological analysis of the real world shows that it is both heterogeneous and united, and the central ontological aporia of the real world is to understand how its deepest heterogeneity does not preclude its unity. The fundamental task of Hartmann's new ontology is twofold. First, it has to discern the basic categories of each stratum. Second, it must determine their mutual relations. The former task is concerned primarily with the categorial differences of the individual strata, the latter with their essential interconnectedness.

Like Aristotle and unlike Kant, Hartmann treats categories as the determinants of the specifics of being, not as concepts of the understanding. In Hartmann's view, Kant does not sufficiently distinguish between our concepts of categories and categories themselves. Categories, in his view, are not mere forms imposed by the mind, nor do they determine in the way that causes, reasons, grounds, or purposes do. They are universal principles of being that have no independent existence aside from the things and events they determine; categories are not applied to reality by the mind but are inherent in things and events they determine.

In two of his ontological works—*The Structure of the Real World* and *New Ways of Ontology*—Hartmann distinguishes the categories specific to each stratum of reality. The categories of the corporeal world he identifies as: space and time, process and condition, substantiality, causality, and reciprocity, as well as dynamic structure and dynamic equilibrium. His categories of animate nature include: adaptation and purposiveness, metabolism, self-regulation, and self-restoration, the life of the species, the constancy of the species, and variations. His categories of the psychic reality involve: act and content, consciousness and unconsciousness, pleasure and displeasure. Finally, the categories of the spirit are: thought, knowledge, will, freedom, judgment, evaluation, and personality. There are no dominant categories within a single stratum, but all of them jointly determine everything. As a result, it is impossible to grasp a single category by itself.

In addition to the categories specific to each stratum, Hartmann detects some categories that run through the entire sequence of strata, although in varying forms. Such categories are: unity and multiplicity, concord and discord, discretion and continuity, substratum and relation, element and structure, form and matter, inner and outer, determination and dependence, identity and difference, generality and individuality, as well as the modal categories and their negative counterparts.

The unifying theme in Hartmann's pluralistic picture of the real world is that of a Heraclitean opposition and dynamic balance. Opposition is not to be confused with contradiction, which Hartmann believes exists only in thought. Every known structure in the real world, from atoms and solar systems, to animals and man, displays a complicated array of counter-forces and always attempts to maintain a balance. For Hartmann, there is no independence without dependence. More precisely, all there is, is partial independence and partial dependence, and they complement each other very well. For instance, there are two ways in which the higher mode of being is dependent on the lower: the first is existential (spirit cannot exist without a supporting consciousness and, indirectly, a body), and the second is limiting in terms of content and structure (the lower mode of being provides matter and serves as a basis for reshaping and rebuilding of the higher form of being). These two forms of dependence can also be used to illustrate the basic laws regulating the mutual relationship of the different strata of reality. They are the law of recurrence, which guarantees a partial continuity between the various strata, and the law of novelty, which ensures diversity. The law of recurrence states that the lower categories penetrate into the higher strata, but not the higher into the lower. The law of novelty pertains simply to the emergence of higher categories into the higher ontological stratum. The determining power of matter does not extend beyond its limiting function; it does not prevent the novelty of the higher form, but rather limits its scope. Thus the real world is not governed either by matter or by spirit. It can be ruled neither from below nor from above, for every stratum possesses, as well as continuity, a certain irreducible specificity. In full agreement with the advocates of transdisciplinarity, Hartmann maintains that the real world is an intricate, perplexing, multilayered, and dynamic unity in heterogeneity.

## III. Included Middle and Transdisciplinary Logic

Hartmann's view that the foundations of logic—its laws and structures—are ultimately ontological rather than mental, should resonate well with Nicolescu's views. The author of *La transdisciplinarité* maintains that it is precisely the acceptance of a more complex, multidimensional reality which allowed Stéphane Lupasco to make a decisive break with the traditional logic of the excluded middle. Nicolescu has in mind the recognition of the coexistence of the quantum world and the macrophysical world, and how that acceptance led to a resolution of what was then considered an intellectual scandal provoked by a number of untenable pairs of contradictories: wave and corpuscle, continuity and discontinuity, reversibility and irreversibility of time, and so on. Although numerous experiments in quantum physics have clearly indicated the simultaneous presence of both elements, these pairs appear mutually contradictory when they are analyzed by classical logic. This logic is founded on three axioms: (i) The axiom of identity: A is A; (ii) The axiom of non-contradiction: A is not non-A; and (iii) The axiom of the excluded middle: there exists no third term T which is at the same time A and non-A.

Lupasco develops the logic of the *included* middle: there exists a third term T that is at the same time A and non-A. He thereby resolved the problems of contradictory pairs, by using the idea of multilayered reality. As Nicolescu explains: "The third dynamic, that of the T-state, is exercised at another level of Reality, where that which appears to be disunited (wave or corpuscle) is in fact united (*quanton*), and that which appears contradictory is perceived as noncontradictory."

Nicolescu points out that although Lupasco's new logic "has had a powerful, albeit underground, impact among psychologists, sociologists, artists, and historians of religion," it has been "marginalized by physicists and philosophers." It may be more accurate, however, to state that philosophers have been too preoccupied with their own objections to classical logic and their own attempts to develop a viable alternative to it.

Let me mention a few examples. The principle of the excluded middle, together with the principle of bivalence ("Every statement is either true or false"), has recently come under attack by prominent logicians and philosophers of language, such as Michael Dummett. The reason for this attack should sound familiar: the dynamic flow of many processes in reality makes it difficult, if not impossible, to establish whether many of our statements are either determinately true or false.

The other two principles, the principle of identity and the principle of non-contradiction, have also been under critical scrutiny for a long time. Hartmann, for instance, challenges the alleged tautological character of both principles. The claim "A is A" is not an empty tautology for it asserts that A is in one certain respect identical with something with which it need not be identical in another respect. The propositions "A is B" and "A is C" do not separate the subject A into two different beings. The real principle of identity should be expressed as "$A_1$ is $A_2$," and this principle is basic insofar as it functions as the ground of any possible judgment.

What Hartmann has in mind in these general remarks may be reconstructed in the following way. What am I doing when I state, for example after we finish a chess game, "These pieces are heavy"? First, I direct my audience toward the definite aspects of the perceptual field and direct attention toward some specific occurrences in it. I thereby establish temporary boundaries of the perceptual field: in this specific case, we are not talking about the weight of the chessboard or about the specific position of the pieces on the board. Second, by means of various concepts I identify the perceived objects as belonging to a certain type of objects (rather than to any other type). Had my intentions been different, these pieces could have been identified not as chess pieces but as pieces of wood, as pieces of different colors and shapes, or as toys with which my children like to play. Had my intentions been different, I would not have focused on that one definite characteristic of these pieces; rather I could have considered whether they are new or old, expensive or cheap, big or small. By asserting that these pieces are heavy, I compare them with and differentiate them from other pieces. Thus, declarative statements always purport to establish what is the case, and this involves identifying what is the case and differentiating it from other things and events. This process is never one of establishing a simple identity (of the kind: A is A) or a simple difference (of the kind: A is not B), but rather of relating different aspects of the same thing to each other: thus: $A_1$ is $A_2$, but $A_1$ is not $B_1$.

Hartmann holds a similar view with regard to the principle of non-contradiction. Considered in itself, it cannot be recognized that "A is not non-A," because every synthetic judgment has the form "A is non-A." Is it evident that A cannot at the same time be B and non-B? Obviously not, answers Hartmann. The indispensability of the principle of non-contradiction is not based on its alleged tautological nature, but again on its function: only under the assumption of its absolute validity can the uniformity of things and judgments be preserved. But whether such uniformity really exists in being or in the logical realm, and whether such a presupposition should, indeed, be taken for granted—that we cannot prove from the principle itself. Nor can we establish it in any other satisfactory way. Just as the principles of knowledge need not themselves be known, the principles of rationality need not themselves be rational.

One of those who seriously challenged classical logic—although he does not get very good press with Nicolescu—was Hegel. The German philosopher clearly recognized that life is not constrained by the principles of logic and that there are oppositions and antinomies everywhere in reality. Any living organism violates the principle of non-contradiction since it simultaneously contains several stages of its development: any growing 'A' is also a 'not-A,' both in terms of embodying a 'pre-A' and an 'after-A.' Hegel captures this idea in the following way: "The bud disappears in the bursting-forth of the blossom, and one might say that the former is refuted by the latter; similarly, when the fruit appears, the blossom is shown up in its turn as a false manifestation of the plant, and the fruit now emerges as the truth of it instead. These forms are not just distinguished from one another, they also supplant one another as mutually incompatible. Yet at the same time their fluid nature makes them moments of an organic unity in which they not only do not conflict, but in which each is as necessary as the other; and this mutual necessity alone constitutes the life of the whole."

It is only when our naturally interactive mind closes itself to the possibilities of a reciprocal relation to reality that it starts imposing its own preconceived and rigid categories onto the world, be they appropriate or inappropriate, or more or less appropriate. But the "all-or-nothing" character of the basic principles of classical logic does not apply well to natural processes, which allow almost infinite shadings and degrees.

As Hegel, Hartmann, Dummett, and other philosophers argue, classical logic should not be confused with "the science of thinking," for the laws of logic are not the laws of our actual thinking. This does not mean that the standard principles of classical logic are false or inappropriate. But it certainly means that we should be far more cautious about the range of their proper application. Nor does this criticism intend to imply that we do not need logic or rationality. If anything, we need more logic and rationality. But we need logic and rationality that are not separated from the interactive processes taking place in reality. We need logic and rationality open to the dynamism of life and willing to participate in that dynamism. This indeed may be the only way for logic and rationality to be of value in our transdisciplinary pursuit of truth.

## IV. Transdisciplinary Epistemology

Of the three pillars of transdisciplinarity postulated by Nicolescu, the third one—complexity—is the least clear. Quantum physics undoubtedly leads us to realize that the universe is far more complex than we have previously suspected, but this insight has already been captured by the first pillar: the fact that reality is multidimensional certainly entails that the universe is a complex whole. The second pillar also implies complexity, this time concerning our thinking about reality. We have seen how some of the principles of classical logic need to be revised, but their revision has to extend also to the—up to now mostly uncontested, yet fundamental—principle of sufficient reason. This principle is one of those that is often used when explaining the overall structure of the universe, but it has also had the most detrimental and arresting effects on our thinking. This is because the principle of sufficient reason tends to turn the world into a closed, static and rationally organized system. But this is not what the world is; the world is full of leaps, as well as accidental happenings, chance, and luck.

To clarify this dynamism, Nicolescu introduces the distinction between "Objective Nature," "Subjective Nature" and "Trans-Nature." I must admit, however, that I have a problem with this triad. Following Lupasco's new logic, Nicolescu somewhat mechanically interprets everything through the prism of triadic relations, without even trying to see whether some relations can be explained in simpler, binary terms. We have already seen in the previous section that even some problems regarding the principle of non-contradiction can be resolved by remaining on the same level of reality.

Regardless of whether we insist on binary, or triadic, or some other kind of relation, the key point still concerns the interactive relation between subject and object, humanity and the world. The mind should not be understood as separated from the body—as has so often been done—nor as separated from other layers and aspects of reality. As a matter of fact, the mind is tied to reality in innumerable ways and functions interactively. As Hartmann expresses it, "man is placed in the midst of the world, and is dependent upon it in incalculable many ways." Just as the senses are capacities for interaction, so is the mind. The mind is the capacity to be open, to interact with perceived differences and grasp their underlying similarities and connections. These differences may originate and be perceived anywhere: in our own thoughts, in our bodies, in other minds and bodies, in the immediate or mediate environment.

Following our previous discussion, the third pillar should be more correctly understood as a transdisciplinary epistemology, rather than as complexity. Based on such an epistemology, cognition itself should be understood as a kind of interaction: a form of interacting with other forms of interaction. In cognitive experience we do not, strictly speaking, respond to individual and isolated objects; we respond to the relations they have with other objects and with us.

How can we go beyond these initial remarks and get a better grasp of what a transdisciplinary interactive epistemology—and accompanying conception of truth—would amount to? Perhaps by pointing out that one of the deepest "truth traps" in past thinking about the nature of truth has been to assume that truth must depend either on the way the world is, or on the way we are and think about the world. But why should that be the case? Since the relation of "being dependent" admits of degrees, in principle it is possible that truth depends both on the way the world is and on the way we are and think about it.

In this respect, all traditional theories of truth are one-sided and inadequate. It is not that they completely miss the nature of truth; rather, they capture only a few of the relevant aspects and disregard all others. For instance, correspondence theories correctly emphasize that truth depends on the way the world is. But they mistakenly separate human beings from the world and alienate thinking and judging from their objects. Thus, they try to define truth as a dubious "pictorial" or "geometrical" congruence between cognitions and objects. Coherence theories, by contrast, correctly emphasize the relevance of our conceptual apparatus and background knowledge. Yet they inflate the relevance of the subjective factors and underestimate the degree to which truth depends on the way the world is. As a result, they sever ties with reality and make true judgments appear to belong to a consistent but perhaps fictional story. Pragmatists correctly underline the functional role of truth, its connectedness to our needs, intentions and goals, and its relevance for practical orientation in the world. But they tend to ignore some of the constraints that exist on the side of the object.

What are those constraints? Roughly speaking, they are the subjective and objective conditions that both create the possibility of objective truth value and impose certain limitations on what is true or false.

Let us first consider the constraints on the side of the subject.

(S1) First, there is a certain plasticity, or flexibility, of the subject. It is manifested by the degree of fluidity or rigidity of the subject's goals, intentions, and expectations. Rigidly defined expectations and goals blind us to certain aspects of situations we encounter. Fluid and flexible expectations and goals make us open-minded to unexpected things.

(S2) Further, there is the question of the respective simplicity or complexity of the subject. This is not measured by the number of components or parts involved, but by the complexity and sophistication of their background knowledge. An amateur chess player would not recognize a certain pattern of pieces as the Sicilian Defense; a person not familiar with chess at all would not even recognize a pattern of pieces as a checkmate.

(S3) Finally, there are constraints having to do with the availability and structure of the cognitive apparatus. Our senses are structured to make only certain dimensions of observed reality accessible. The nature of our intellectual abilities similarly opens some vistas and closes off others.

What about the constraints on the side of the object? The senses provide the needed cognitive material which, when properly formed, allows for cognitive contents and judgments. The material provided by the senses—the underdetermined objects of empirical intuition—has the potential to be determined in various ways. But these underdetermined objects must also impose some limitations on the possibilities on the formation of objectively valid judgments.

Here are a few such constrains.

(O1) One concerns the plasticity, or the level of underdetermination, of the observed objects or events. A simple curved line is normally more plastic than an equally simple straight line. The shape of a cloud is more plastic than the shape of a square. All objects and events have their own specific degrees of plasticity which function as limiting factors in our attempts to perceive and grasp those objects and events.

(O2) Then there are constraints that deal with the respective simplicity or complexity of objects or events we try to grasp in our cognitions. Objects and events contain more or fewer components. A geometrical figure involves more components than a straight line; a chessboard involves more components than one of its squares. More complex objects and events offer more resistance to our attempts to grasp and illuminate them.

(O3) There is also a level of relative accessibility or inaccessibility of observed objects or events. It is easier to grasp one billiard ball hitting another, than the action on a football field; it is easier to grasp a straightforward opening move in chess than one that starts a complex combination. Even without attempting to postulate about invisible essences of things, it may be that there are layers of reality that are—temporarily or permanently—inaccessible to all of our cognitive advances. As Heisenberg sums it up, following Frances Bacon and Kant, "We have to remember that what we observe is not nature in itself but nature exposed to our method of questioning."

If we want to express the interactive relation between these subjective and objective constraints in a more formal manner, we could evoke Bertrand Russell's famous propositional function: 'f(x).' The subjective constraints listed above are roughly analogous to the function 'f,' and the objective constraints are represented by the variable 'x.' The subjective and objective elements permeate each other and interact in order to create judgments with a determinable truth value. More generally, thought and being are different in the way 'f' and 'x' in the interactive propositional function 'f(x)' are different. "Different," however, does not mean completely ontologically and functionally independent and separate from one another. Rather, 'f' and 'x' work together and create a certain harmony. Although distinguishable, 'f' and 'x' need each other and depend on each other. Kant's famous dictum concerning concepts and intuitions finds its full application here: functions without variables are empty, variables without functions are blind. It cannot be said that one is more important than the other, or that one dominates the other: they simply have different roles, and one without the other is incomplete. Only in their interaction can they fully realize their potential and fulfill their roles.

Questions of truth and falsity became dependent on the presence or absence of a harmonious relation between 'f' and 'x,' and truth itself can be defined as their harmonious interaction. This means that our statements (judgments, propositions, theories) are true when (i) we recognize the challenges posed by the situations in which we find ourselves [the interaction element], and (ii) we respond to the spirit of the challenges we face [the harmony element]. By contrast, our judgments can "go wrong" for two different reasons. They are false (mistaken, erroneous) when we respond inappropriately and violatively to the task at hand [interaction but no harmony]. They are illusory when, blinded by our own conceptions, interests or ideals, we do not recognize the challenges posed by the situations in which we find ourselves [no interaction]. Harmony and disharmony clearly allow of degrees. An interaction can be more or less harmonious. It can also be partially harmonious and partially not. In which case, truth and falsity are, in reality, extreme values or points on a scale that contains many intermediate shades and possibilities.

## V. Toward a Transdisciplinary Theory of Values

Transdisciplinarity is more than a method. It is more than a guideline for conducting research and collecting knowledge. When Nicolescu names one of the introductory chapters of the *Manifesto* "Tomorrow May Be Too Late," he voices a concern shared by many about the direction in which our fragmented sciences and, indeed, our whole disoriented civilization is going. The overwhelming response to the outcry of the *Manifesto* is the best evidence that Nicolescu's concerns are shared with many other scientists, artists, and intellectuals.

Nicolescu argues that the "potential for self-destruction—material, biological, and spiritual—is the product of a blind but triumphant techno-science, obedient only to the implacable logic of utilitarianism." Almost a century ago, Albert Schweitzer—one of the true predecessors of transdisciplinarity—similarly diagnosed the decay of our civilization by pointing out that the "interaction of material and spiritual has assumed a most unhealthy attitude." Transdisciplinarity intends to correct this imbalance, not only by emphasizing the inalienable rights and values of the inner person, but also—very much in the spirit of Schweitzer—by reestablishing our sense of wonder and reintroducing our appreciation for the sacred. The sacred is not to be understood in a strictly religious sense, since transdisciplinarity aspires to be transreligious, just as it attempts to be transcultural and transnational. Transdisciplinarity aspires toward the establishment of a harmonious coexistence with living Nature.

There is a problem here, however—not with the transdisciplinary vision itself, but with its full articulation and realization. Even Nicolescu himself does not seem aware of the magnitude of the problem, since he does not find it necessary to establish a fourth pillar of transdisciplinarity, one that would deal with values and their systematic examination. The issue is that we cannot get very far with the declaration that transdisciplinarity affirms the presence of the sacred, or that transdisciplinarity strongly favors rigor, openness, and tolerance, without a methodical discussion about what the sacred involves, as well as a systematic inquiry into how the sacred relates to other values and endeavors. Similarly, rigor, openness and tolerance are steps in the right direction, but we also need a fully developed map of values and a comprehensive examination of their nature.

Surprisingly, when we look back at the history of our civilization, it is hard to find any discipline more neglected, and involving more prejudices and confusions, than that of axiology, i.e., the philosophical study of value. The Greek word *axios* means "being worthy" or "estimable," and it has the same roots as two words with which we are, perhaps, more familiar: *axon* and *axioma*. *Axon* is translated as axis. Taken literally, *axon* refers to the straight line, real or imaginary, that passes through a body, and around which it revolves, or may be imagined revolving—the earth's axis, for instance. Taken symbolically, "axis" refers to a turning point or condition, around which something (say, our lives) may turn and on which it may depend. *Axioma* is the Greek word from which we get the term *axiom*. It means authority, or an authoritative sentence. A combination of these words can indicate how values function as well as how they relate to facts.

Values are not facts; they are not an ontological Atlas on whose shoulders the earth stands. Rather, they provide a center which gives us a sense of orientation. Values provide an axis of orientation for our lives, for our attitudes and deeds, for our decisions about what is right and wrong, valuable or not. Values also provide an authoritative voice guiding us to make proper choices concerning how to live our lives and develop our humanity.

Considering how important axiology is, why is it one of the least developed disciplines? A full answer to this question would demand a long and detailed study. For a short answer, it may suffice to point out that we often forget the wisdom behind the old proverb "a stick always has two ends," on which Nicolescu relies in his explanation of the central tenets of transdisciplinarity. Throughout the history of our civilization, values and facts have frequently been contrasted, and some thinkers have attempted to derive one from the other. One prototype, the Platonic, has been advocated by idealists of various schools. According to this view, values are ideals that transcend facts and beings, and facts and beings are real only to the extent that they imitate and participate in those ideal values. The second exemplar is the reversal of the first and has been championed by proponents of modern science (empiricists, positivists, and pragmatists). In this view, facts and beings are higher than values, and values either derive from facts, or must at least be justified by facts. There have also been those who realize that the stick must have two ends, and that all attempts to derive values from facts, or facts from values, must be futile. The efforts of Max Scheler and—even more so—Hartmann must be mentioned here, though their works create a puzzling conundrum, since for both of them, facts belong to the real world, and values to the ideal, but it remains unclear how they relate to and interact with each other.

Circling back to our previous discussion, I believe that a transdisciplinary theory of values must also be based on an interactive relation of facts and values. How does this work, though? We have already indicated that the basic function of the mind, when judging the world and collecting knowledge about it, is identification. We need to identify what we observe by classifying it and recognizing both how similar and how different it is from other things and events we observe. When we deal with values, on the other hand, the basic function of the mind is orientation. Values function like a coordinate system for the map of reality we are trying to assemble. Values do not elucidate what is and what is not, but only what is valuable and what is not. Since they have different functions, the relationship between facts and values is not hierarchical, nor can one be reduced to, or derived from the other. Their relationship is dynamic, reciprocal, and mutually supportive. Their relationship is interactive.

We are still far from any developed transdisciplinary and interactive theory of values, but the skeleton of such a theory need not be so obscure. For such a theory to succeed, it must overcome three main challenges. First, it must explain the nature of values, by contrasting them to non-values (such as facts), and by showing how they are mutually related. One would need to figure out the ontological status of values, as well as whether and how their validity can be objective. Second, it would need to clarify the nature of values by explaining the contrast between positive and negative values, as well as between various kinds of positive values. It would also need to clarify, more specifically, the distinction between intrinsic and non-intrinsic (or instrumental) values, and the distinctions between means and ends on the one hand, and parts and wholes on the other. Third, and perhaps most importantly, it would need to elaborate on the nature of values by examining possible conflicts between various positive values. The plurality of values would also need be considered, in its various aspects. It is not just that we need to distinguish between moral and non-moral values; it would be useful to establish a full scale of values, as well. We might never locate an *a priori* fixed scale, such as the one Scheler believed he had found, when he distinguished between pleasure values, vital values, spiritual values, and the values of the holy. Nevertheless, more flexible and changeable comparisons of values would be incredibly useful.

These comparisons could be especially useful when dealing with certain unavoidable disputes between positive values. In the face of the threatening dilemmas we confront both as individuals and as a civilization, it is of utmost importance to learn more, not only about whether and how such conflicts arise, but also about whether and how they can, in principle, be resolved. One of the deepest problems of our time is the problem of orientation—the problem of choosing and pursuing the proper way of living. This problem is intensified and magnified not only because of our real potential for self-destruction, but also because of a lack of universal values and a depreciation of the spiritual and the sacred. In the absence of any appreciation of such values, in the absence of any clear vision of a new art of living, and the lack of the kind of genuine commitment that would put a free and spontaneous development of individual personality at the center of all values, we are walking a dangerous tightrope. As Nicolescu puts it: "We have not advanced at all on great metaphysical questions, yet we permit ourselves to intervene in the very depths of our biological being. In the name of what?"

Nicolescu puts his finger here on something extremely important. However, he does not go deep enough in dealing with the issues involved. Of course, considering how serious the threat of self-destruction is, his question, "In the name of what?" is by no means rhetorical. Taking into account the fact that, as a civilization, we have neither the insight nor the courage to understand and confront our bleak predicament, the possibility of our collective self-destruction seems even more threatening than the prospects of genetic engineering. If we are realistic and serious, we have every reason to suspect that humanity will self-destruct. Taking into consideration our apathy, moral cowardice, culpable ignorance, and deadly weaponry, and factoring in the effects of increasing ecological degradation and the unstoppable demographic explosion, it is not at all improbable that humanity will not survive beyond the twenty-first century.

Yet this is not a black or white, either-or situation. At issue is not a choice between a negative value on one hand, and its opposing positive value on the other. The dilemma involves choices between various positive values. There are potential answers to the question: "In the name of what?"—even if we don't find all these answers satisfactory. Options include: in the name of human curiosity; or in the name of increasing our power over people and the ability to control and manipulate them; or in the name of short-term gains; or in the name of curing curable diseases; or, more generally, in the name of idealistic attempts to "fix" those human faults that perhaps could be corrected by means of genetic engineering.

As in all truly difficult dilemmas, the choices have to be made between diverging positive values. And these choices are all the more difficult to make, because we have not advanced at all toward resolving the great metaphysical questions, such as: Is the world fully rational? Is there a higher meaning inherent in the world and its events? What if the world is partially (or completely) irrational? What if there is no higher (or any other) meaning inherent in the world and its events?

We could continue to expand this list of great metaphysical questions which we still have not answered, and, if we keep in mind the real possibility of self-destruction, the list would also have to include various questions concerning the value of human life: Does human life have an intrinsic, or absolute, value? While it is clear that, *prima facie*, life is a value and death is disvalue, it should also be clear that we may overestimate the value of life (e.g., when health is taken as the highest good and a vital value is placed too high, beyond its proper measure), and also that we can underestimate its value (e.g., when all value is posited as existing exclusively in the life beyond, as in various forms of asceticism).

Our dilemma is additionally complicated by two further factors. The first is that, throughout history, humanity has not really succeeded in reforming itself and the battle to improve humanity has never been won. The second, also pertaining to history, is that it is quite possible that the deep and genuine conflicts between values can never be resolved, and we should renounce the ideal of a unified hierarchy of values.

Keeping these issues in mind, we can more clearly see the different kinds of complications behind Nicolescu's concerns. In the name of what, he wonders—justifiably—are we risking the biological restructuring, or even the destruction, of the human race? Yet, as long as we lack satisfactory answers to the aforementioned metaphysical questions, we can also ask (with equal justification, and similar confusion): In the name of what should humanity be preserved and kept intact?

These concerns make it more obvious, I hope, why we need a transdisciplinary theory of values, and also why such a discipline is of such crucial importance. How else could transdisciplinarity, understood as a comprehensive approach, even attempt to bring us closer to a genuine resolution of these and other difficult metaphysical questions? How else would we prevent a new and revolutionary movement, which we now call transdisciplinarity, to turn into just another one of those countless "isms" it is supposed to replace? How else would we avoid being disappointed one more time, by yet another illusory hope and unfulfilled promise? The relevance of transdisciplinarity, as well as its fate in the future, will depend on whether it can provide satisfactory solutions to these genuine and disturbing puzzles.

As Nicolescu correctly observes, our situation is truly paradoxical: "Everything is in place for self-destruction, but everything is also in place for positive change … The global challenge of death has its counterpart in a visionary, transpersonal, and planetary consciousness, which could be nourished by the miraculous growth of knowledge. We do not know which way the balance may swing."

Indeed, we do not know which way. Nor do we know whether we have the courage and wisdom to reawaken our sense of wonder and our appreciation of the sacred, to dedicate ourselves toward building a new kind of humanity. If we do not find out soon, tomorrow may be too late.

# 5. Being Human:
# On the Puzzling Value of Human Life[1]

*Shifting the discussion toward a comprehensive examination of values, in this essay I examine our opposing attitudes regarding the value of human life. While the main issue initially appears to be whether or not human life has an intrinsic (or absolute) value, it turns out that a far more important and complex issue has to do with the tension between the belief that all human life is of equal value, and the reality of differences in quality of life. Following a discussion of the views of Kant, Schweitzer, Berlin, Scheler, and especially Hartmann, I do not offer a simple response to the challenge of determining the value of human life. The puzzling and complex issue of the value of human life is a reflection of the puzzling and complex nature of humanity in general. Thus, we need to reexamine our vision of what human life is about and what it means to live like a human being. Following Hartmann, I challenge the reader to consider whether we can believe that there is something good in each of us and whether we can still find enough inspiration to strive, in our own ways, toward that which is great and superior.*

Regardless of our culture, gender, or age, we humans seem to hold an array of incompatible attitudes about the value of human life. Sometimes we go out of our way to fight for and preserve every single life; other times we are completely indifferent to the fact that people who could be saved are left helplessly dying. We display the same ambiguous attitude toward our own lives: sometimes it appears that they are more valuable to us than anything

---

1    Originally published as "On the Puzzling Value of Human Life," in *Ethics and Bioethics*, 7:2017, No. 3–4, pp. 155–68.

else, while in other circumstances we are ready to sacrifice our lives for some higher value.

It would be unreasonable to claim that human life has no value whatsoever, yet when it comes to establishing precisely what value it does have, we typically have no answer. This perplexity may not be accidental; it may be an indication of our inability to demonstrate the value of human life in any conclusive manner. Or it may be an indication of the complex nature of the value of life, and perhaps of other values as well. It remains to be seen which of these is the case. What is clear is that we are facing a challenge. As Max Scheler formulated it in *The Human Position in Cosmos*, "Man is more of a problem to himself at the present time than ever before in all recorded history."

To prod deeper into this problem, let us focus our inquiry on the following four statements:

(1) Every human life has an intrinsic (or absolute) value.
(2) No human life has any intrinsic (or absolute) value.
(3) Some human lives are more valuable than others.
(4) No human lives are more valuable than others.

By the "value" of something we mean its worth. However that worth must be specifically defined. To say that a being's value is intrinsic is to maintain that this being is desirable and esteemed for its own sake, for its own inherent qualities. Similarly, a value of something is absolute if it is never relative to any other condition, restriction, consideration, or circumstance.

Can such an intrinsic and absolute value be justifiably ascribed to human life?

Our initial reactions to this question are probably going to be ambiguous, for such a claim appears both intuitively evident and too strong. Following the history of the twentieth century—which may be called the century of genocide—we would like to affirm that all human life is valuable in itself. This holds true not only for extraordinary human beings, or even for every normal and healthy person. Rather, it is true about *every* human being: a premature baby who is going to live for a few hours only, a starving child in India or Somalia, a homeless person on the street of New York or San Francisco, or an Alzheimer patient dying secluded in some nursing home. Every one of these individuals is unquestionably valuable and every one of them should be given a chance to live and die with dignity.

These are inspiring thoughts. But irritating doubts will always manage to creep in: What could possibly rationally justify this view that every human being is sacred and of unquestionable value?

If we are willing to admit that *prima facie*, every human life is a value and death is a disvalue, what other value but intrinsic (or absolute) could we wish to ascribe to human beings?

In *An Analysis of Knowledge and Valuation*, C. I. Lewis distinguishes between the following values:

(i)   utility or usefulness for some purpose;
(ii)  instrumental value (of means);
(iii) inherent value (or goodness);
(iv)  intrinsic value, or being desirable as an end or in itself; and
(v)   contributory value, relevant for our understanding of the relationship of parts and whole.

While these distinctions are easily comprehensible and, in many contexts, useful, they are not much help for our discussion. Clearly, we are not going to claim that the value of human life is any variety of (i), or (ii), or perhaps even (v). But on what grounds could we argue in favor of (iii)? And perhaps most importantly for our discussion, how can we establish—or, conversely, refute—that (iv) is the case?

Before we attempt to answer these questions, we should be aware of three potential ambiguities. The first is that value is usually ascribed to objects and acts: we say that a book has some (determinable) value, and that giving it to someone as a gift is a valuable act. Yet, life cannot be counted as either an object or an act. This anomaly may be one source of our difficulties, but it may also lead to unexpected new insights.

The second point is that we need to be careful not to confuse the so-called "vital values"—such as health, energy level, life-enthusiasm, and so on—for the "value of life." Vital values deal with values vital *for* life, while our topic is about the value *of* life.

The third thing to remember is that we are asking not merely whether we should regard human life as inherently and intrinsically valuable. For our interpersonal relations it is very useful, of course, that we do regard each other in that way. Yet, just as there is a meaningful distinction between assenting to something as true and the question of its truth—and the two need not overlap—a similar distinction holds good here. So we need to ask, also: Is it true that human life really has such an intrinsic (and absolute) value?

## I. Does Human Life Have an Intrinsic Value?

The central issue here seems to pertain to the question of whether (1) or (2) is true: Does human life have an intrinsic (or absolute) value, or does it not?

The view that every human life has an intrinsic (or absolute) value has traditionally been supported on two principal grounds, one religious, and one moral. Considering the religious ground first, it is plausible to argue that the central message of the gospel is the sanctity of all human life. But why would this be the case? Does the gospel reveal some undeniable facts about human nature based on which a special value of human life can be posited? Is there something about the origin of humanity that would automatically reveal its preciousness? Furthermore, if one takes this line of reasoning about the sanctity of human life, why not go a step further and claim, together with Albert Schweitzer, that not only human life but all and any life is precious? As God created human life, He has also created all other life.

Schweitzer religiously inspired reverence for life—*Ehrfurcht vor dem Leben*—suggests that good consist in maintaining, assisting, and enhancing life, and that to destroy, to hurt, or to hinder life is evil.

While Schweitzer's line of reasoning appears deeply admirable, it has found few adherents. We can agree with him that life is more valuable than death, and that we should avoid unnecessary destruction of human and all other life. Yet, one can have a solemn reverence for the miracle of all life without asserting that all life is sacred, or that it has an intrinsic (and absolute) value. Not surprisingly, in his practice as a physician Schweitzer had to recognize that, in order to preserve and enhance some life, other lives must be destroyed. Thus, his principle should be interpreted as primarily directed against our mindless and often unnecessary destruction of life.

66

Moreover, if we were to argue that not only human life but all life is sacred, why not make an even bolder step and maintain that every being, everything that exists at all, is precious and sacred? The reason we do not maintain this is that, despite a deeply embedded Platonic and Augustinian tradition, we do not believe any more that "being" implies "goodness," or that "non-being" implies "evil." More generally, "existence" does not imply "value," and "non-existence" does not imply "disvalue." By the same token we can claim that "life" does not imply "value," and "death" (or "absence of life") does not imply "disvalue." Our great teacher Socrates taught us long ago that fear of death is irrational and that only the good life (and not mere life, nor life in every form) is worth living.

We may thus be advised to see whether the claim that every human life has an intrinsic (or absolute) value can be supported on some other, perhaps moral, grounds. Kant argues, for instance, that every human being is an end in themself and should never be treated as a means only. This so-called second formulation of the categorical imperative offers one of strongest supports for the view that human life has an intrinsic (and absolute) value, but it also leads to numerous questions and concerns. Kant is right to claim that the value of human life should not be considered in terms of instrumental values alone; but does it make sense for him to thus ascribe an intrinsic value to human life? I do not think so, and for the following reason.

Suppose we approach the world with a noble ideal that every human being is an end in themself, and treat every person accordingly. Like the Christian precept to love our neighbors as we love ourselves, Kant's categorical imperative, were we to implement it in this way, would probably make the world a better place. Yet it would also lead to some maddening dilemmas. There is no problem in treating as ends in themselves our neighbors who behave reasonably and morally. But can we—and should we—treat murderers, rapists, and violent maniacs in the same manner? Should we treat them as rational moral agents even when they behave both irrationally and immorally? Should we treat them as having intrinsic value as ends in themselves even when their behavior threatens not only our existence, or the existence of those who are dear to us, but the existence of humanity at large?

To be fair to Kant, he himself wavers between praising humanity as an end in itself and complaining that of "such crooked wood as man is made of nothing perfectly straight can be built." He never successfully reconciles these diverging views. Nor would that be an easy task to accomplish. Kant would have perhaps strengthened his cause had he more clearly distinguished between the value of human life *in general*, and the value of human life *in concreto*. The latter is a matter of specific appraisal and cannot be resolved by any *a priori* decree. But what exactly could, and should, we say about the value of human life in general? Just as in his theoretical philosophy Kant tries to put an end to "the scandal of reason" by offering a conclusive proof of the existence of the external world, in his practical philosophy Kant attempts to remove an analogous scandal by demonstrating an intrinsic (and absolute) value of human life.

Perhaps, in both cases, Kant's approach is misguided. We do not really need a proof of the existence of the external world, because the presupposition of its existence belongs to the very framework of any intelligent discourse and cognition of reality: it is necessarily presupposed for any cognitive experience. It may similarly be beyond the power of our mind to prove that humans are of some ultimate, intrinsic, or absolute, value. But such a proof may not be needed either. The value of human existence seems intuitively obvious to us.

We have feelings for values. It is true that such feelings may be more or less developed, and that their accuracy and depth may vary. It is also true that the presence of such feelings does not demonstrate that the value of life is intrinsic; it only shows that such a value exists and that it is significant. This value is significant not only because it helps us establish a respectful attitude toward other human beings, but also because of the function this value has in our overall valuational experience. Namely, the value of human existence belongs to the framework within which all other values can be experienced and realized.

Human beings are the bearers of values. One could even argue that, for all we know, the non-human world is devoid of values. In which case, just as the external world is an indispensable arena for any cognitive experience, human life is a needed battlefield on which the claims of conflicting values in concrete human lives can be adjudicated. As a value, human life may well be indefinable, but it provides a presupposition for the realization of other values, and perhaps also a framework within which different kinds of values—e.g., pleasure values, goods as values, vital values, spiritual values, and values of the holy—may be related, assessed, and realized. This may not be what we initially wanted in order to support claim (1), but it may be one element of that view, that has yet to be fully developed and defended.

## II. At the Crossroads

Just as we, in Western civilization, have, thanks to our Christian heritage, developed attitudes of compassion and high esteem for every human life (claim 1), we can trace our strong support for the view that some human lives are more valuable than others (claim 3) to our Greek ancestors. With their ethics of aspiration, the ancient Greeks were preoccupied with striving toward virtue and excellence. For them life was both a struggle with oneself and a competition with other human beings. Philosophers such as Socrates, Plato, and Aristotle came to understand, however, that the fundamental task is not to compete against others and make ourselves better than them. Rather, it is to compete against ourselves and to become as good as we can possibly be. Instead of an "egalitarian" ethics (based on equality), the Greeks believed that we should endorse one based on merit (or quality).

We can strongly object to the vulgar ancient division between "civilized Greeks" and "uncivilized barbarians," as well as reject the Greeks' treatment of those human beings they considered "slaves by nature." Nevertheless, we can also maintain that, in terms of numerous specific values, some human lives can, indeed, be viewed as more valuable than others. We are different not only in terms of inborn capacities and gifts, but principally in how far and how completely we develop and exercise them. How we live cannot be disregarded, for those ways of life make our lives more or less valuable. The *quality* of life must be taken into consideration when we discuss what value human life may have.

We have now arrived at the central crossroads in our complicated aporia concerning the value of human life. The real challenge consists not in the opposition between (1) and (2), but in that between (1) and (3). The primary conundrum regarding this axiological aporia is whether we should accept one of them—either one—or whether accepting any one of them may be both extreme and unsatisfactory, so that a proper response to the challenge can only consist in some kind of reconciliation between (1) and (3).

Consider the reasons for choosing either (1), the claim that every human life has an intrinsic value, or (3), that some human lives are more valuable than others. It appears that, just as a consistent Christian would be opposed not only to (2) but also to (3), a consistent advocate of the Greek ethics of aspiration would have to dispute not only (4) but (1) as well. The reason for this becomes clearer if we make a more general distinction between "having a value" and "being given a value": if all things are in themselves already valuable, there would be no sense in attempting to make them valuable. Thus, the tension between the view that every human life has an intrinsic (and absolute) value, and the view that some human lives are more valuable than others is real; this controversy not only characterizes our age but belongs to the very core of Western civilization.

As the tension between claims (1) and (3) is real and important, so are the various attempts to resolve it. Even though Christianity clearly favors (1) over (3), its rich and complex tradition indicates a number of ways in which they can be reconciled, including the simultaneous emphasis on mercy and compassion, on the one hand, and the project of *imitatio Dei*, which is essential to our humanity, on the other.

Following Jesus, Schweitzer believes in the affirmation of all life. But inspired by Goethe and Nietzsche, who were motivated by ancient Greek traditions, Schweitzer also believes in a continuous effort toward ennoblement; our ideal must be to deepen our moral life and express it in moral action. Kant similarly believes, if not in the *Grounding for the Metaphysics of Morals* and *Critique of Practical Reason*, then certainly in his later work *Metaphysics of Morals*, that our two fundamental goals in life are the perfecting of ourselves and the happiness of others. This civilization has generally believed that to strive toward what is noble and good, toward the highest values and aspirations, is fundamental to human nature. So, from this perspective, the view that some lives are more valuable than others (claim 3) is more intuitively clear and seems to need less rational grounding than the view that every human life has an intrinsic (or absolute) value (claim 1). Nevertheless, taken to an extreme, this view may lead to something like Nietzsche's devaluation of all "pity" and the reaffirmation of the ancient Greek ideal of excellence in terms of his *Übermensch*. Such an extreme view appears intuitively mistaken, just as much as does its counterpart, which denies any morally relevant sense in which human lives are not equal.

70

## III. Scheler's Scale of Values

If these extreme views are both equally unacceptable, our inquiry has come to the following point: claims (1) and (3) stand in a clear opposition to each other. Plus, taken in isolation and driven to an extreme, they seem not only one-sided, but incomplete and, ultimately, unsatisfactory. Is there, then, any hope that, despite that opposition, and despite our tendency to swing from one extreme position to another, they may be reconcilable? Max Scheler's views on values, together with his famous scale of values, may offer a way out of this aporia.

For (1) and (3) to be compatible, some kind of commensurability between these rival claims would be needed. The main challenge, then, is to locate a suitable ground for their potential and fruitful commensurability. Minimally, we need to assume that both are true, then show how both can be true in different domains, or different ways. From here, the crossroads may take us in two distinct directions. The first, which Scheler pursues, would entail showing that there is a unified, or one-dimensional, scale by means of which the value of human life can be precisely determined.

Scheler believes in an objective order of higher and lower values and tries to establish a one-dimensional scale that could reveal the exact standing of each value on that scale. The hierarchy of values is itself absolutely invariable, but the order of preference in history is variable. Scheler also realizes, however, that no matter how that scale is constructed and used, we always run into counterintuitive examples: the value of human life cannot be permanently situated at the top of the hierarchy of values, nor at its bottom, nor even somewhere in the middle.

Scheler attempts to address this problem by adding several additional categories and formulating a complicated law of preference, but his successors abandoned this project. Even if we accept that every human life is *prima facie* valuable, can we properly estimate the value of each life without taking into account an individual's deeds and attitudes? And when we take them into consideration, we run into a plurality of values, some apparently incompatible with others, and with no definite hierarchy. A value of human life may be not only indefinable but also indeterminable in any *a priori* manner. If so, this would account for both the richness of human life and for the bewildering difficulties we encounter when attempting to properly

71

estimate its worth. Does this mean we can make no further progress beyond the realization of the plurality and complexity of values?

A paradoxical thing about Scheler's thought is that, despite his conscious effort precisely to establish the value of human life, he would in many ways welcome our conclusion; it may well be consistent with some of his other fundamental views. For instance, in opposition to Kant's rigid formalism, Scheler's moral theory is based on the view that our experience of values is not discrete but contextual. Rarely, if ever, is a value given in isolation from other values, and we always evaluate things within the given situational background, as well as within the background of our own social and personal experience. Before we can make a rational choice, there is a lot we must know, and even when we know as much as possible, the tip of the scale may still stand pretty close to a dynamic equilibrium. Or it may not even be clear in which direction it points. Of course, in practical life a choice still has to be made, for even a refusal to choose is itself a decision that carries with it inevitable, frequently undesirable, implications and consequences. Whatever choices we end up making, we are not only in a double bond but in a double bind as well.

Some moral philosophers may be disappointed by this line of reasoning; they may insist that moral theories are designed to tell us how we ought to act and what kind of attitude we should assume toward our lives and lives of others. But how can we expect a more principled theoretical solution when there is a divergence between (1) and (3)?

Scheler might answer that we can still offer a variety of "maxims" and "rules" of prudence concerning our own lives as well as the lives of others, but this will not necessarily bring us any closer to a principal solution to our problem. For if we reject moral theories that postulate absolute obligations and prohibitions, we find that no moral theory can regulate all possible cases. As Scheler points out, theories and norms are too abstract and remote from actual ethical situations; they are disembodied and impersonal, too detached from the dynamic of real life.

This lack of a principal position on the value of human life may be the result of our indecisiveness, however, or of our inability to approach these ethical issues in a systematic and thorough manner. But it could also, on the contrary, be precisely the result of a realistic assessment of human nature and the complex role that human life plays in reality. Our very nature may be too convoluted; we may be pulled, simultaneously, in many different direction and attracted toward inconsistent values, so that an adequate principal position is not possible. The values themselves are not necessarily obscured, nor is the problem that we have an imperfect vision of them. It may be that choosing between them, and choosing rightly, is what is so difficult—and so distinguishably human.

Robert Nozick, with his attempt to balance what he calls the "moral pull" and the "moral push," puts forth a similar position. So does Isaiah Berlin, who recognizes the irreconcilable oppositions of some fundamental values, such as equality and liberty, order and tolerance, justice and mercy. Unlike Nozick, however, Berlin perceives this predicament in a pessimistic manner. We are doomed to choose, in his view, and every choice may entail an irreparable loss: "If, as I believe, the ends of men are many, and not all of them are in principle compatible with each other, then the possibility of conflict—and of tragedy—can never be wholly eliminated from human life, either personal or social."

Must the conflict of values have such pessimistic implications, though? No, it does not, according to a fascinating, although undeservedly neglected, approach which we can find in Hartmann's *Ethics*. In this masterpiece, first published in 1926, Hartmann accepts as many (if not more) conflicts of values as does Berlin, yet he argues in favor of (i) the plurality of values, (ii) their absoluteness, as well as their mutual (iii) irreducibility, (iv) partial incompatibility, and ultimately their (v) potential synthesis.

## IV. Hartmann's Account of Values

Following Scheler, Hartmann maintains that values are essences, in the phenomenological sense of that word. Values, in his view, possess the character of genuine essences, that is, absoluteness, and any knowledge of them must be aprioristic knowledge. Values have their own ideal self-existence: their realm is not of real but of ideal being. That means, among other things, that values are not only independent of the things that we estimate as valuable; they are their prerequisites: things can be valuable only through a relation to values themselves. It also means that values are equally independent of persons, who cannot make or create values. Nor do values change as a result of a person's insights.

Against Scheler, Hartmann maintains that our understanding of values in general, and of the worth of human life in particular, can be further advanced if we recognize a two-dimensional scale of values. In accord with his ontological views, Hartmann contends that values can be meaningfully contrasted not only in terms of their respective height but also with regard to their strength; instead of one kind of "bond" between values (respective height), he postulates two (height and strength).

Like the ontological strata of reality—and Hartmann distinguishes between four of them: the inorganic, the organic, the conscious, and the spiritual—values are structured from bottom up. Stronger values serve as a foundation for weaker values, but the positive reinforcement of stronger values does not thereby bring higher values into existence. Higher values have at least partial autonomy with regard to their lower counterparts.

The key point for Hartmann is that the highest values are the weakest, and that the strongest values are the lowest. Higher and weaker values are dependent for their realization on the realization of lower and stronger values. Lower values are thus the *conditio sine qua non* of higher values and become "matter" for them, or their "clay to be shaped." Despite such conditioning, the specific form of such shaping is introduced by higher values and cannot be predetermined by lower values.

The value of human life in general definitely belongs among the most basic and foundational, i.e., the strongest and the lowest values. Higher values are those of the personal subject, and they are not universal but individual values. The strength and relevance of the strongest values is expressed through prohibitions, and it is not accidental that every society considers the murder of other human beings as one of the worst crimes. Notice, however, that there is an asymmetry with respect to violation versus positive reinforcement of values: although murder is among the worst kind of violations, respect for life does not thereby automatically represent a very high value. Furthermore, a violation of a lower value is a greater offense than a neglect of a higher value. Nevertheless, a realization of a higher value is more valuable than a realization of a lower value.

Hartmann formulates this relationship as the "inverse law of strength and height," which fully captures the double bond of values: evidence of strength is found in the seriousness of the offense against a value, while height is known by the meritoriousness of fulfillment. Our moral project can be summed up like this: do not violate the stronger values and do aspire to realize the higher values.

Where does this approach leave us with our concerns about the value of human life?

First, it makes us aware not only of the plurality but also of the interconnectedness and multidimensionality of values. More specifically, it cautions us against thinking of human life in terms of one single value that could be artificially isolated and separately defined. There are many values we associate with human life, and this richness is also indicated through the difference between two relevant expressions: "human being" and "being human."

Claim (1) is closer to the former expression and claim (3) is more focused on the latter. "Human being" (like "human life") refers to something that is given, a *datum* of a kind, while "being human" refers to a task—it points to the incompleteness and under-determinacy of the *datum* and poses a challenge to us. Human beings have a strong desire not only to live but to live well; we have a deep awareness of the insufficiency of sheer living, and the question for us is not only whether to live but how to live. Provided that existence is granted, there is no excuse for failing to try, as seriously as we can, to bring about that which we consider to be good, beautiful, and true.

Different cultures and viewpoints would understand this task of self-realization in diverse ways. Our Christian and Greek ancestors, for example, conceived it in different fashions and were pointing in divergent directions. As a result, we have inherited internally conflicting ideals and value systems.

There are different reasons for clashes of values. The most obvious reason is an enormous plurality of values; Hartmann, in what is published in English as the second volume of his *Ethics*, considers more than forty different values. In his view, although values can be systematically analyzed, they cannot be arranged on a single scale of values. Instead of one single valuational scale which ascends in a series, or a pyramid of values with one highest value, Hartmann presents a network of multiple, frequently mutually dependent but also inconsistent values that he compares to a starry sky.

When he speaks about inconsistences and conflicts of values, Hartmann does not have in mind an opposition between one positive and one negative value (as in [1] and [2], or [3] and [4]). We always choose among things we find valuable, so the real divergence of values is either between two positive values (as in [1] and [3]), or between two negative values. To be more precise, when we experience a conflict of values it is either an oppositions between values themselves, or a conflict of various situations in which we attempt to actualize values.

Only conflicts between values themselves can lead to what Hartmann calls "antinomies of values." He offers numerous examples of such antinomies, but for our present purposes it suffices to mention just one: the value of the communal versus that of the individual, and related to this, the conflict between the general equality all human beings share, versus the specific inequalities arising from different persons having different individuating characteristics.

Hartmann's most original treatment of the antinomies of values is to be found in his view that there are four equally fundamental and mutually irreducible moral values: the good, the noble, the rich in experience, and the pure. The good is characterized by striving toward the highest value, and by attempts to covert values into ends. The noble is the value of the pursuit of one value to the exclusion of all others. Richness of experience is the value of personal many-sidedness, including some things that cannot be estimated as good; it is radically opposed to the one-sidedness of the noble. Purity is founded on single-mindedness and opposed to the richness of experience; unlike the noble, however, purity is predicated upon obliviousness to the opposition inherent in the good and noble character.

In addition to pointing out that these four fundamental moral values are not mutually consistent, Hartmann maintains that the entire realm of values is characterized by ineradicable tensions and anatomies between values. Moral life is life in the midst of conflicts and life itself presents the greatest challenge for man as a spiritual and valuational being.

Like Berlin, Hartmann maintains that there is no pre-given schema for determining how such discrepancies of values should be handled; every individual, facing these conflicts, has to rely on their own sense of value as well as their personal preferences. Hartmann surprises us, however, when he points out that the existence of antinomical tensions is itself valuable; such tensions keep our discernment of value alive and help further sharpen and develop our feeling for it.

Unlike Socrates, who continually battled against human ignorance and misconceptions, Hartmann is more focused on the narrowness of our "value-horizon": most of us basically sleep-walk through life, oblivious to its complexity and depth, indifferent to the richness of values. Our blindness toward the higher values impoverishes us and prevents us from living authentic human lives. To a value-blind person, everything ultimately becomes worthless, even that which is valuable in itself. But to the open-hearted man, by contrast, everything is valuable, even what is in itself seemingly contrary to value. "There is certainly no other way to ethical maturity and expansion than through the conflicts of life itself, through "moral experience"—even experience of wrong-doing, and this perhaps most of all."

Conflicts and antinomies of values are not, for Hartmann, tragic since they help us to awaken our value-feelings and value-intuitions; they convey to us a sense of amazement and respect for a cosmos rich with values. Hartmann is a genuine pluralist about values, but he is not a relativist. He believes in the universality, necessity, and objectivity of valuational judgments. But not everyone has the eye, the ethical maturity, and the spiritual development for grasping the structural relations of values or for judging valuational situations as they truly are. The maieutic function of philosophy is thus to free us not only from ignorance but also from our "passing by values," and our indifference to them.

Besides pointing to strength and height, as two respective ways of comparing values, Hartmann also discusses the idea of a synthesis of values. While Berlin laments what he calls "the incommensurability of values," Hartmann reminds us that no single value exists for itself; rather, every value finds its fulfillment only in its synthesis with other values, and—finally—in one Idea, in one synthesis of all values. Such synthesis is not something given, but rather an ideal toward which we must all strive: "Only a sense of justice which is at the same time loving, only a brotherly love which also considers the far distant, only a pride which would likewise be humble, could be valid as an ideal of moral conduct."

The synthesis in question does not pertain to the relations among values themselves. Rather, it concerns their actualization. The lower values as such do not antagonize the higher; it is only a preference for their actualization which clashes with a preference for the actualization of the higher.

In our moral thinking, no less than in our moral practice, we tend to pursue single values, often to an extreme extent. Hartmann warns us that such extremes serve only to distort our sense of values and misguide us into one-sidedness. The real challenge is to ground our moral and spiritual lives on a solid foundation of lower values, for only in the synthesis of strong and high values we can find the reciprocal content of both types of values. To discern their synthesis, however, is a far more difficult task than that of attaching oneself exclusively to one side and disregarding the other: "The secret of human progress is that advance must be along the whole line, and not by fragments, that the trend towards the highest must be accompanied by a trend toward the most elementary. Every other progress is only a semblance. It surrenders on one side what it wins on the other."

## V. Hartmann on the Value of Human Life

Hartmann does not offer a simple solution to the challenge of determining the value of human life. His views are nevertheless beneficial, not only because of their originality, but because they help us discern our proper place and role in reality. The puzzling and complex nature of the value of human life is a reflection of the puzzling and complex nature of values in general. More specifically, Hartmann's perspective could be summed up as follows:

First, there is a fundamental antinomy in the nature of values: there is a claim to validity that goes in two opposite directions. Our unconditional preference for the higher is restricted by an equally unconditional preference for the lower and more fundamental values.

Second, life is a value and death is a disvalue. Life is not created by human beings, but it exists, it is real, and it is given to us; life is, as it were, entrusted to our care.

Third, we may overestimate the value of life (e.g., when health is taken as the highest good, then a vital value is promoted too high, beyond its proper measure), and also underestimate its value (e.g., when all value is posited to reside only in the life beyond; that is, asceticism).

Fourth, there is a value particular to life itself, and it may well be an intrinsic value. An intrinsic value does not, however, have to be the highest value.

Fifth, life itself is not the highest value, but it is a very significant value; it is a foundation of all higher values. The value of life does not disappear

78

just because it is not linked with some higher values, e.g., values of spiritual existence. Nonetheless, life gains a decidedly higher significance from being connected with such spiritual values.

Let us revisit once more our original claims, in light of Hartmann's understanding of values.

(1) Every human life has an intrinsic (or absolute) value.
(2) No human life has any intrinsic (or absolute) value.
(3) Some human lives are more valuable than others.
(4) No human lives are more valuable than others.

While (1) refers to the value of life itself, and (3) refers to the quality of life, (2) and (4) are not their negations. Rather, they direct us toward those positive values that make the transition from mere life to quality of life possible. Such an understanding of these claims (1–4) captures Hartmann's view that there is something good in each of us, and that we all, in our own ways, strive toward what is great and superior. And this striving is perhaps the most beautiful feature of humanity.

# 6. The Value of Money: Finding the Proper Measure[1]

*In our consumerist world, our values center around the possession*
*of money and the possibility of buying things we never before imag-*
*ined we needed. Shopping has become our lifestyle to the extent that*
*our sense of freedom seems to be reduced to a choice between brands.*
*This state of affairs can be examined from three perspectives: apolo-*
*getic, critical, or through an attempt to balance our obsession with*
*money and shopping with a proper understanding of higher values.*
*Following Hartmann, I develop the last of these standpoints. We*
*should not be too concerned about our love for shopping, nor is there*
*anything wrong with convincing people to buy things they never*
*imagined they needed. But it is problematic when we spend more*
*time shopping than with our children and reorganize our schools*
*as if they were corporations created to make profit. The problem of*
*our age is that we place money, shopping, and economic values on*
*a pedestal that is inappropriately high: we see the highlights of our*
*lives in terms of shopping and the acquisition of new things, while*
*in reality the values of these experiences are far lower. The central*
*task of our age is to find the right balance between low and strong*
*material values on one hand, and high and weak spiritual values*
*on the other.*

On September 9, 1869, Aristide Boucicaut laid the foundation stone of what
would soon be hailed as the greatest department store in the world, the Bon
Marché. He thereby launched a new era of consumerism, which altered our
perception of the hierarchy of values and our conception of the good life.
Boucicaut transformed a few filthy streets of Paris into a fantasyland, where

1    Originally published as "Finding the Proper Measure: The Value of Money
     Versus Higher Values," in *Ethical Thought*, Vol. 20:2020, No. 2, pp. 132–44.

the culture of limitless desire could run rampant. The Bon Marché was designed to get people to buy things they had never imagined they needed. It redefined shopping as a lifestyle and freedom as a choice between brands. Since 1869, if not earlier, money has been treated as if endowed with an ethical value: a prosperous way of life signals worthiness, while a lack of money is treated as though it indicates some practical or even moral deficiency.

Almost a century and a half later, this fantasy continues. The consumerist fever does not reveal any sign of waning; quite the contrary, it may be at its zenith. Recent surveys show that Americans spend an average of six hours per week shopping, but less than 40 minutes a week playing with their children; in comparison to 50 years ago, the time an average American adult spends shopping is nine times that which they spend playing with their children. Based on the latest statistics from the U.S. Department of Commerce, the average American makes over 300 trips to the store annually, spending close to 400 hours per year shopping. Assuming a typical life span, this would amount to 8.5 years of life spent occupied with shopping.

Higher education in the U.S. is among the most expensive in the world, yet annually Americans spend more on shoes, watches, and jewelry (around $100 billion) than on higher education. Since 1987, shopping malls outnumber high schools in the U.S. At the beginning of 2020, there were around 26,000 high schools and 5,300 universities and colleges in the country. By contrast, there were 38,000 supermarkets in the US. They offer over 25,000 items for sale, including around 200 different kinds of cereal and a staggering number of 11,000 magazines.

At the end of 2019, U.S. retail sales were over $5 trillion, and total retail sales across the globe reached over $27 trillion. The world's biggest retailer is Amazon.com, and it is nowadays as much of a "landmark" across the world as the Bon Marché was in Paris in the late 19th century. Appropriately, the founder and CEO of Amazon.com, Jeff Bezos, is the wealthiest man on the planet: at the end of 2017, he surpassed Bill Gates (the founder of Microsoft) with a net worth of 91.6 billion dollars. During the COVID-19 pandemic, which has devasting the world in terms of human and economic loss and which has already left dozens of millions of people without jobs, Bezos has virtually doubled his wealth, which in May of 2020 is estimated to be around $150 billion. (Bill Gates is ranked second, with the "paltry" $106 billion.)

Although at least one half of the world's population lives in poverty and deprivation (on less than $2.50 a day), plenty of us are privileged to live in this culture of excess that stimulates "limitless desire" and enables us "to buy things we had never imagined we needed." Money gives us a sense of power and increases our feeling of self-satisfaction. Not surprisingly, then, the slogan in our consumerist world is "shop 'til you drop."

## I. Defending Money-Based Materialism

If during a shopping adventure we were to slow down before dropping, we might realize that in this culture, only money is worshiped as sacred. Although money is nothing but a substitute for real goods, it is treated as though endowed with quasi-religious qualities. Even our personal relationships have become centered around money, and our worth is estimated by how much money we possess. If we could sustain our thought process a bit longer, we might also question whether things ought to be this way. Why do we, deep down, have such a strong, lingering, and unpleasant feeling that this situation is wrong? And not just wrong, but bordering on perverse and sick?

Could it be, though, that our negative feelings and intuitions regarding the worship of money are outdated and unjustified? Perhaps the way things are is just the way they should be. It is certainly possible that where we stand now is just a phase in our civilization's development and there may be a rational explanation for why we have reached this stage. If we view things from a historical perspective, we might realize that we should not worry so much about our consumerist fever or our adoration of money. After all, we shop and we consume because we can. And more people can do this in our time than ever before in the history of the world. Why not, then, just enjoy the moment?

I find this line of thought proposed in a currently popular book by Yuval Noah Harari, *Sapiens: A Brief History of Humankind*. In a short period of time—the book was first published in Hebrew in 2011, then in English in 2014—it has been translated into 50 languages and has become an international bestseller, with over 15 million copies sold. Harari reconstructs our human history within a framework provided by the natural sciences, particularly evolutionary biology. One of his central ideas is that "sapiens" managed to survive and came to dominate the globe because they are the only animal that can cooperate flexibly within large numbers. This ability to cooperate in large numbers arises, according to Harari, from our unique capacity to believe in things existing purely in our imagination.

In chapter 10 of this book, entitled "The Scent of Money," Harari reiterates that the emergence of money "involved the creation of a new intersubjective reality that exists solely in people's shared imagination." Like gods, nations, and human rights (among others), money is not a material reality but a psychological construct. Money is not coins and banknotes. It is anything that people are willing to use to represent the value of other things for the purpose of exchanging goods and services. To illustrate this, Harari maintains that the sum total of money in the world is estimated to be about $60 trillion, but the total of its "material representatives"—banknotes and coins—is less than $6 trillion. More than $50 trillion of this money exists only in our accounts. In other words, more than 90 percent of all money exists only on computer servers.

The key to the working of money is that it is a universal medium of exchange that enables people to convert almost everything into almost everything else. This near-universal convertibility creates, claims Harari, a special kind of trust: "Money is accordingly a system of mutual trust, and not just any system of mutual trust: money is the most universal and most efficient system of mutual trust ever devised." The crucial role of trust explains why our financial systems are so tightly bound up with our political, social, and ideological systems, which in themselves are not directly related to economic values; it also explains why financial crises are often triggered by political developments, and why the stock market can rise or fall depending on numerous events seemingly unrelated to strictly economic issues.

Harari is well aware of our intuitions that connect money with something unworthy, even dirty: for centuries, intellectuals have reviled money and even considered it the root of all evil. Harari maintains that this attitude is deeply unfair. In contrast to the entrenched view, he considers money as the apogee of human tolerance: "Money is more open-minded than language, state laws, cultural codes, religious beliefs, and social habits. Money is the only trust system created by humans that can bridge almost any cultural gap, and that does not discriminate based on religion, gender, race, age, or sexual orientation. Thanks to money, even people who don't know each other and don't trust each other can nevertheless cooperate effectively."

And just when we think that money has found the latest among its growing number of unapologetic advocates, Harari cautions his reader about the "dark side" of money: "For although money builds universal trust between strangers, this trust is invested not in humans, communities or sacred values, but in money itself and in the impersonal systems that back it. We do not trust the stranger or the next-door neighbor—we trust the coin they hold. If they run out of coins, we run out of trust. As money brings down the dams of community, religion, and state, the world is in danger of becoming one big and rather heartless marketplace."

But why would we need hearts (or souls), a true believer in money could ask, if the marketplace keeps our egos inflated and satisfied? Before we deal with this question, we should examine Harari's views about money as "the apogee of human tolerance" and "the only trust system that can bridge almost any gap between human beings."

## II. Money as the Symbol of Impersonality

Instead of promoting money to the status of absolute good and encouraging the worship of the "Golden Calf," it is more appropriate to compare money with the grammar of a language. As with any grammar, what is important is not tolerance or trust, but rather structure and stability. Grammar gives us rules for the correct use of a certain language, and provides a foundation for the translation of that language into any other. Grammar is an instrument and should not be glorified for anything other than serving its proper function. Nor should money. Neither grammar nor money has any absolute (or intrinsic) value. The sentences of our language can be grammatically correct or incorrect, but, once we realize that they are correct and thus capable of general communication, the question shifts toward their meaning, and the value of what is being said. The situation is analogous to that of money, except that the mistake of treating money as an absolute value has more fatal consequences for the quality of life and future development of humanity.

In his critical commentary, Harari points toward one of the fundamental problems with money: money exchanges depersonalize human relations. Money is a symbol of depersonalization. Before we got so involved in money transactions (in our age, by means of bank or phone transactions, or credit cards, without handling any actual money), people used to engage directly in the exchange of goods. They used to relate directly to each other, so the distance between them was far narrower than it is today. From the literal exchange of goods, which in most cases people produced themselves, we switched to exchanging money for goods. That gift of exchange still required interaction and a direct relatedness to another person, however. The currency, originally an extension of such relatedness, gradually became its replacement, its substitute. We have come to the point at which the producer and the customer never come face to face with each other. They often have no knowledge of each other, and do not care to have any. Direct relatedness and exchange have turned into money transfers and money transactions, which eliminate the need for any personal relationship. We have certainly gained something in the process, but we have lost a lot: the gift of human contact and human concern.

What Harari considers as "tolerance" and "trust" are veils over indifference and mistrust. As long as a customer has money, we disregard the questions of how the money and the product to be purchased are obtained. We also ignore the question of who wants to obtain the product and what they intend to do with it. We turn a blind eye to the persistent links of trade and finance on the one hand, and violence and crime on the other.

In *Debt: The First 5,000 Years*, David Graeber discusses the unpleasant details associated with the criminalization of debt, which ultimately led toward the criminalization of society as a whole. Behind a banker there is almost always a man with a gun. Behind an industrialist, an army of mercenaries. What began as the search for spices (by Spaniards and Portuguese) settled into three broad trades: arms trade, slave trade, and drug trade (including coffee, tea, sugar, tobacco, distilled liquor, opium, and other drugs). Graeber does not attempt to discuss explicitly how we arrived at the point of a systematic criminalization of society characterizing our age. Instead, he stresses that what in earlier times was considered as one of the greatest vices—greed—in modern times is hailed as "self-interest" and "ambition." What may look, in various business places, like welcoming smiles and genuine care for the customer is nothing but purely impersonal relations centered on money, numbers, contracts, credits, statistics, spreadsheets, and, ultimately, the making of profit: "The moment that greed was validated and unlimited profit was considered a perfectly viable end in itself, this political, magical element became a genuine problem, because it meant that even those actors—the brokers, stock-jobbers, traders—who effectively made the system run had no convincing loyalty to anything, even to the system itself."

Whether or not God cannot create something out of nothing may be up for debate, but successful merchants, bankers, and financiers certainly seem able to do so! Inspired by Goethe's *Faust*, Graeber calls these individuals "financial alchemists" and "evil magicians." Although written decades before the opening of the Bon Marché, Goethe's *Faust* anticipates the modern financial "alchemism," which Goethe calls by another name: our bargain with the devil. Graeber maintains that, although most of us may not yet be aware of it, this bargain leads toward several deeply problematic changes that profoundly affect every level of society, undermine our humanity, and lead to the decline of civilization.

We can consider these changes via the following five insights. First, money can turn morality (and any other aspect of human life, including faith and trust, love and accountability) into a matter of impersonal arithmetic. Due to the overwhelming dominance of economic values, even the language of morality becomes increasingly reduced to the language of business deals.

Second, the whole spectrum of human relations becomes a matter of cost-benefit calculations. Modern capitalism has created social arrangements that force us to think this way; it is essentially a structure designed to eliminate all imperatives but profit and consumption.

Third, in business transactions, everyone is treated as a stranger. Non-personal relations and values are treated as more desirable than values pertaining to human personality; the instrumental values assume the role of absolute values. Even though they are put on the highest pedestal, such values have no stability, just as they have no intrinsic value: what matters is what is desired, what is in demand, or what is fashionable—but that can change from year to year, from month to month, or even from day to day.

Fourth, money and power are the inventions of distrust, not of trust. To compensate for the lack of trust, the fetish of money and power are always backed up by some violent force, rather than with an increased attitude of personal responsibility and accountability. Since everything depends on numbers and the use of force, the fetishization of money and power represents an escape from personal responsibility and avoidance of accountability.

Fifth, capitalism is a system that demands constant and endless growth. It pumps more and more labor out of everyone with whom it comes into contact, and as a result, the value of material goods is endlessly expanding. On the other hand, capitalism is also a system that refuses to address certain basic questions about its own value: What are these goods for? Can they really replace what has been lost in the process of increasing growth and focusing on making more profit, namely the quality of personal relations and personal values?

While Harari paints a fairly optimistic picture regarding our passion for money and shopping, Graeber believes that our predicament is much graver than we realize. We know how much things cost, and what it takes to purchase them, but we do not know what things are worth. We see wealth displayed and praised, but ignore what stands behind its acquisition and accumulation. Capitalism seems to lead toward the destruction of all higher values and the prosecution of human personality, yet we do not seem to see, or search for, any viable alternative.

## III. Resolving Value Conflicts

Graeber compares the predicament of the modern man to that of Goethe's Faust, but seems to overlook that Faust, in Goethe's version of the story, is not doomed. Faust is saved because of his genuine and relentless striving toward the highest values. Graeber explains neither why Faust (and the rest of us whom he represents) makes a bargain with the devil, nor what values Faust (and the rest of us) should strive toward. On these points we benefit from the perspective of Hartmann, who does not see our predicament as either entirely hopeless or entirely positive. Although he lived before Harari and Graeber, Hartmann balances out the extreme positions later defended by them. He offers a healthier view of the proper place and role of money and commerce in our lives as well as a positive view of what we should strive for.

While money is certainly unlike chairs and houses and similar material things, Hartmann is more cautious than Harari about declaring that it exists only in people's imagination. He is even more circumspect concerning the claim that values belong to this same category of imagined things: values, for Hartmann, are not fictions or psychological constructs; they are ideals and our principles of orientation. Values are ideal beings, in distinction from real beings (such as chairs and houses and similar material objects).

Furthermore, Hartmann holds that values have objective validity, which is not dependent on our opinions. To be truthful, for instance, is valuable, whether or not others recognize that we are such, and even when they think that we are not. Truthfulness is valuable regardless of how the society in which we live regards it. Values themselves are not relative, but our judgments of values may be relative: our judgments may change, or they may be reversed, but that does not affect the status of the values themselves.

One of the most important insights of Hartmann's monumental *Ethics* is his realization that we operate with two irreducible scales of moral values. We wish to have one unified scale of values and we behave as if there were only one scale—as Harari and Graeber certainly do—but this is not realistic. I reality, we have one scale which deals with values' respective height, another which has to do with their respective strength. Some values are high, such as the value of personal love, trust, purity, and nobility. There are, conversely, low moral values, such as justice, solidarity, self-control. and modesty. The crucial point is that, while both scales are used and needed, there is a reverse relation between them. The lower values are the stronger values: they are stable and foundational. By contrast, high values are normally weak: they are unstable and not necessary for the maintenance of life. Nevertheless, the lower and stronger values are as indispensable for moral life as the higher and weaker ones.

If there were only one scale of values, our choices would be much simpler. But with two scales, things get complicated, and conflicts between values become far more difficult to resolve. When facing a conflict of values, we need to realize that whatever value we favor, we automatically reject its contrasting value. Regardless of whether our choices are between two goods or between two evils, the very nature of moral life makes it impossible for us to be guiltless. No one should be blamed for this guilt, nor can it be removed by any scapegoating sacrifice: it stems from the nature of our moral predicament and the moral universe itself.

Since moral conflicts are an integral part of reality and since we operate with two scales of values, we need to realize that some present genuine antinomies which do not admit of a rational (either-or) resolution. For example, the values of freedom and security stand in such a relation to each other; their discord between these two values arises from their very nature. Other conflicts are created when we attempt to realize both values under specific circumstances and at the same time. In certain situations, for instance, it is possible to favor self-control over courage or the other way around, but it may be impossible to realize both at once.

The third kind of conflict between moral values is of the greatest interest in our present context. It deals with the issue of the violation of value versus the fulfillment of value: If we must choose between the violation of a stronger but lower value and the fulfillment of a higher but weaker value, how should we resolve this dilemma? Hartmann's view is subtle and his asymmetrical treatment of values deserves our full attention: "To sin against a lower value is in general more grievous than to sin against a higher; but the fulfillment of a higher is morally more valuable than that of a lower. Murder is held to be the most grievous crime, but respect for another's life is not on that account the highest moral state—not to be compared with friendship, love, trustworthiness ... A sin against the lower values is blameworthy, is dishonorable, excites indignation, but their fulfillment reaches only the level of propriety, without rising higher. The violation, on the other hand, of the higher values has indeed the character of a moral defect, but has nothing degrading in it, while the realization of these values can have something exalting in it, something liberating, indeed inspiring."

Hartmann's other example, which is of even more interest in our context, deals with private property. Private property is an incomparably lower value than personal benevolence, but none the less a violation of property (theft) is much more reprehensible than mere malevolence. Despite favoring higher values, Hartmann's view does not imply what some great figures from Plato and Jesus to Tolstoy and Gandhi have insisted on, namely that we should consider private property as something to be repudiated. Even less does it imply that private property is evil.

Hartmann develops his idea about the two scales of values primarily by considering the conflicts between moral values. However, as this last example suggests, these ideas apply to non-moral values as well. The economic values (including the value of money) are strong, but not high. These, for Hartmann, are low values, located toward the bottom of the second scale of values. Thus, in this paradigm, money—and economic values in general—cannot provide life's crowning achievements; still, they can serve as a foundation for our overall social life. What Harari calls trust (regarding money) is really reliability, that is, our capacity to make promises that others can be sure will be respected, and the violation of which people know will be dealt with adequately, according to standard practices or previous agreements.

Generally speaking, personal values (such as trust, faith, and personal love) are high but weak. Hartmann maintains that trust (properly understood) is one of the highest yet also one of the weakest moral values: "All trust, all faith, is an adventure; it always requires something of moral courage and spiritual strength. It is always accompanied by a certain commitment of the person. And where the trust is far-reaching, where the faith is impregnable, there the commitment is unlimited, and with it the moral value of the trust raises proportionately."

Hartmann's analysis also helps us put Graeber's criticisms into the right perspective. Graeber argues in favor of a system of relations that would be the opposite of financial relations, but mainly defines it in negative terms, insofar as it is envisioned as being the opposite of (financial) debt. Hartmann connects trust with (spiritual) indebtedness, with being indebted to someone for something. Trust thereby is treated as standing outside the categories of the exchange economy. Trust is not a matter of exchange but a gift, and a precious one. This gift, claims Hartmann, is comparable to that of love, and as a value, can even transcend it: "The ability to trust is spiritual strength, a moral energy of a unique kind. Its foundation is not experience, not previous testing. For it is only by showing trust that a man can be tested; and doing so presupposes that spiritual energy. Faith exists prior to experience. It alone is the foundation of genuine trust. What justifies such faith is only a sensing of moral value in the person."

Like Faust, we need to strive toward the values of personality, which deal with the development of one's general human and uniquely individual potential. The values of personality are high but weak. They need the support of the more fundamental, i.e., strong and low, values, and economic values are of this kind. Personality consists not only in freedom to choose a course of action, to foresee, but also in the capacity to be the bearer of values. As far as we are aware, the human person is the only being in the world capable of the response which gives meaning to value, yet one person requires the loving response of another for the realization of the unique value they bear.

In moral thinking, and in moral practice, each person tends to pursue one single value. Whether it be it love, happiness, equality, or money, everyone is inclined to place this one value on the highest pedestal. But this one-sidedness only distorts our sense of values and blinds us to the richness of life. Hartmann warns that "fanaticism" for any single value—be it higher or lower, stronger or weaker—is dangerous; even the highest values can be poisonous when pursued to an extreme. One's moral life is perverted if one fixates only on the highest values and neglects the lower, as if it were possible to actualize the former while they float untethered and without foundation. At the same time, one's moral life is impoverished when one confines one's moral purpose to the lower values and spends one's life pursuing only them. A morality which is reducible to the values of self-control and justice easily becomes pharisaical; it exhausts itself in safeguards against crime and lower orders of business; even the spiritual freedom which it acquires becomes empty. But morality which only accommodates and fosters the values associated with personality becomes dangerous; it destroys the very ground in which personalities grow. Hartmann concludes: "The fulfillment of the meaning of humanity is never to be found in the foundations of human life; but the possibility of actualizing that meaning is never attached to its positive contents alone. Its aims should be placed so high that man can only just discern them, but its foundations should be laid as firmly as ever they can be laid."

The ultimate challenge, then, is to ground our moral and spiritual lives on a solid foundation of lower values, and then pursue the highest values. Only in the synthesis of strong and high values can we find the reciprocal content of both types. To discern their synthesis, however, is a task of far greater magnitude than that of simply attaching oneself to one side and disregarding the other. In Hartmann's words, "The secret of human progress is that advance must be along the whole line, and not by fragments, that the trend toward the highest must be accompanied by a trend toward the most elementary. Every other progress is only a semblance. It surrenders on one side what it wins on the other."

## IV. Searching for the Proper Measure

If Hartmann is right, we should not be too concerned about such things as the opening of the Bon Marché or our love of shopping. Nor is there anything particularly wrong with getting people to buy things they had not previously thought they needed. But it is problematic that we spend so much more time shopping than playing with our children, and that we obsess over accumulating wealth while neglecting humane values and personal development. It is also alarming that we are trying to reorganize all our cultural institutions, schools and universities included, as if they were corporations created primarily to make profit.

One central problems of our age is that we assign a dangerously high importance to money, shopping, and economic values. There are three respects especially in which we need to find remedies for our unhealthy obsession with shopping and money: one is urgent, and the others have to do with finding long-term solutions to these problems. The issue requiring an urgent remedy is connected to the fact that the modern Faustian individual is a creature of excess and exaggeration. Money makes us desire even more money. We have become convinced that more is always better, with no limit in sight. This attitude lacks moderation and balance and ignores the question of the proper measure. Finding that proper measure is one of the most challenging tasks in life, as it requires knowledge and understanding, together with maturity and resoluteness.

While the idea of finding the proper measure is ancient, it has been especially elegantly expressed by Michel de Montaigne and Blaise Pascal. The elegance of their approach consists in the fact that both thinkers used a single French word to express the idea of the right measure: *portée*. This word literally means the reach of an arm, the range of a weapon, the significance of an event or idea. In his *Essays*, Montaigne discusses the idea of the right measure in the context of his criticism of pretentious knowledge, and presumption in general. He understands *portée* in terms of grasping our limitations and discovering the proper significance in all things. In his *Pensées*, while discussing "man's disproportion," Pascal uses *portée* in a similar way: let us learn and respect our limits. We are capable of many things, but not all. Nor are all these things of which we are capable are desirable. We can obtain many things, but some are harmful. In our age, so dominated by extremes and exaggerations, our sanity and perhaps our very existence may depend on whether we can grasp our own limitations and find the right measure in everything we do—from money-chasing and shopping to the highest personal pursuits and devotions.

We need to think about two other issues, also. One of these deals with the proper understanding of freedom, and the other with the restoration of ideals associated with the most humane way of living. Freedom should be understood, not as a matter of choosing among various options, but as living in a certain way and following certain values. It should be understood as presupposing a moral vision, or a set of ideals, of what it means to live as a human being should live. Understood in that sense and liberated from the narrow conception which reduces freedom simply to a set of free choices, we can appreciate freedom as a supreme gift that only human beings possess. It is the gift that not only points toward the highest humane and personal values but also grounds and enhances our pursuit of these values.

Civilizations have been struggling with the proper understanding of such values for at least the past century and a half. Yet in our pursuit of this understanding, we receive very little help from our political, cultural, intellectual, and scientific leaders, or from our dominant institutions (including those of higher education). In the absence of anything to look up to, we are seduced by the glittering lights of department stores. In the absence of a leader worthy of our trust and faith, admiration and emulation, we make our next choice on Amazon.com.

Hartmann argues that what we lack is an ethos of an "upward gaze." In his words, "In life there is always something to which a man can look up. The upward gaze is not a result, but a cause. It does not arise out of comparison, but itself selects the points of comparison. In the ethos of the upward gaze all reverence and awe have their basis, as everyone who is morally unspoiled proves by his reverence and awe for real worth and merit, for antiquity or for persons in positions of higher responsibility."

The first assumption of the ethic of the upward gaze is that there is something good in every human being. This is the ideal that needs to take the place of the shrewd impersonal calculations of our business transactions, the ideal that could lead us to regain trust and faith in other human beings. This trust and faith can potentially transform every human being, toward

93

either good or evil, according to the moral vision they follow and the highest values they pursue. This is the secret of trust and faith, their power to "move mountains" (as St. Paul expressed it), to lead us toward the vision of a great and upward striving on the part of humanity. Although we should certainly have the time and opportunity to visit shopping malls and purchase unnecessary things on Amazon.com, our central commitment must be to the improvement of the human condition, the development of our personal values, and our common life with others.

# 7. The Spirit That Kills Not:
# Hartmann and Berdyaev[1]

*One major point of difference between Kant and Hartmann is that while Kant does not have a conception of spirituality, in Hartmann's philosophy it plays a central role. Spirituality is broader than morality. If we were to represent it as a circle, it would encompass not only our moral but also our religious experience. This essay first outlines a brief history of different concepts of spirit in the Western tradition, and then offers a more detailed explanation of how spirit is understood by Hartmann and Berdyaev. For both thinkers, freedom, love, truthfulness, and brotherhood are those spiritual values that can lead us away from apathy and corruption, violence and killing, and guide us toward more humane lives. Moreover, both argue that we should further develop this concept of spirit in terms of personality: to be a human being means to strive toward becoming a fully developed person.*

The human person is a spiritual being. While not merely or exclusively a spiritual being, nevertheless, it is spirituality that defines the human individual the most—or perhaps, in the present time, the lack of spirituality. Perhaps more precisely, what defines human existence in our epoch is a confusion about what spirituality is, and a resulting disorientation about who the human person is and what it means to be and live like a human being.

To understand how we came to be so confused about our spirituality and identity, let us briefly consider the history of our understanding of

---

1  Originally published as "The Spirit That Kills Not," in *Nonkilling in Spiritual Traditions*, ed. Joám Evans Pim and Pradeep Dakhal (Honolulu: Center for Global Nonkilling, 2015), pp. 37–52.

spirit, tracing this history back to the beginning of the twentieth century. Then we will pay special attention to the views of Nicolai Hartmann and Nicolas Berdyaev, two philosophers who discussed the concept of spirit in great detail—even in this century that seems to have forgotten about spirit—and who tried to awaken us to its vital significance. At the end, following some suggestions of Hartmann and Berdyaev, I will offer a constructive suggestion as to how to better live in accordance with our true, spiritual nature.

## I. Four Stages in the Understanding of Spirit

One way we can present the history of our understanding of spirit is by distinguishing between its four different conceptions in the Western tradition: 1. the early mythological and poetic tradition of ancient Greece; 2. the later Greek philosophical tradition; 3. the Christian conception; and 4. the post-medieval (or modern) conception. The development winds from conceiving spirit as something almost material, toward understanding it as almost completely mental. But let us go step by step.

If we look for the Greek term of which our word "spirit" is a translation, we find two: *pneuma* and *nous*. *Pneuma* has physical overtones, and literally means "wind" or "breath." Occasionally, it also meant "fire," or "blood," or "blowing of the wind." The concept of spirit, then, originally referred to something dynamic, always in motion and transforming, not tied to any space, nor shaped into any substantial form. *Pneuma* is what comes and goes, an animated and invisible force, whose physical manifestations we can see and need to learn to manage or control. Reality is comprised of two contrasting elements: the world-body and the world-spirit. The world-body consists of objects and things that fill space, while the world-spirit consists of forces that shape the relationships of those objects and things, that glue them together, or keep them away from each other. Where the spirit is present, there is a force that connects, while the absence of spirit means separation and fragmentation.

With the development of Greek philosophy, the shift was made from *pneuma* to *nous*. Philosophers like Plato and Aristotle do not deny the existence of *pneuma*, but they see in it a lower principle. Every living being is a body that contains a breath of life (*pneuma*), but in the world there is also a structure—a law (*nomos*) that regulates the movements of even the seemingly irregular blowing of *pneuma*. Spirit thus becomes a kind of ideal foundation of the world.

Greek philosophers conceive of the world as a *kosmos*, a living organism governed by an eternal and unchangeable law. Not accidentally, the first philosophical discipline was cosmology—an attempt to uncover and explain this hidden law governing every phenomenon of the *kosmos*. The law itself is rational; it is an intellectual code that must, in principle, be knowable. Spirit is thus conceived as a divine revelatory principle, operating simultaneously within the natural world and within the human mind. Philosophy becomes a concentrated and systematic effort to grasp, articulate, and explain the law governing the daily breathing of the *kosmos*.

Under the influence of Socrates, his successors understood "spirit" not only in a cosmological but also in an ethical sense. The *kosmos* is not just governed by the unchanging law that establishes a harmonious co-existence of worldly things. The *kosmos* is also something good. To be, to exist—as opposed to not to be—is something good. The Greeks believed that the *kosmos* has an inalienable ethical dimension built into its core. The Socratic shift toward living a virtuous life is thus not merely an individualistic endeavor, as it later becomes in modern philosophy (decisively so with Kant). For the ancient Greeks, as in certain Asian spiritual traditions, to be virtuous was to live in harmony with the *kosmos* as a whole. Indeed, spirituality itself is precisely manifested in that harmonious interaction of man with the world. Spiritual life is life in accordance with the cosmological and ethical *logos* governing the world.

When spirit is understood as *pneuma* in the Greek mythological and poetic tradition, the *kosmos* and our life in it is usually conceived of in a monistic way: there is *one* principle permeating and governing the entire *kosmos*. With the addition of the ethical element, this monism of some of the early Greeks becomes untenable. As it was clear to Socrates, and as elaborated by Plato and Aristotle, the dynamic balance may be interrupted; the natural world is not always overlapping with the social world. The harmony between the two is not an established fact but more like a desired goal. As Plato's *Republic* and Aristotle's *Nicomachean Ethics* and *Politics* show, the task is to realize that harmony in an individual as well as in a social life.

The Bible returns to and affirms a higher significance of *pneuma* than of *logos* (*nous*)—although *logos* is not forgotten either. In Genesis, God is depicted as animating Adam with a breath. Yet this God—Yahweh—is also the supreme law-giver and law-enforcer. In the New Testament, the transcendent Father connects with his creation through his Son. The Son becomes a historically tangible manifestation of the *logos*. As expressed in the opening sentence of the John's Gospel, "In the beginning was the Word."

This *Word*—or *logos*—is now understood as an eternal truth that has been present from the creation of the world, with a twist that it is now being sent forth in a human form. The Son of God shows us the way toward a unification of the eternal and the temporal, the one and the many. The ethical element is strongly present in the Christian tradition as well. The mission of the Son of God is to awaken all humankind to their true and higher destiny. Thus, the spirit in Christianity is manifested not only as the Holy Father and the Holy Son, but as the Holy Spirit as well.

The Latin term *spiritus* means "breath," "courage," or "vigor." It preserves ties with both *pneuma* and *logos* (*nous*), and in addition has a complex relation with another key concept: that of *anima* (soul). Terminologically, there has always been a distinction between soul and spirit; a verbal distinction between them exists in all Indo-European languages. (In Hebrew, they are *rauch* and *nephesh*; in Sanskrit: *prana* and *akasha*). Speaking metaphorically, the relationship between spirit and soul is analogous to that of blood to the human body. Yet the conceptual connections between them are complex and difficult to completely untangle. Besides the tradition of ascribing spirit to a living person, there is also a longstanding belief in the continuity of spiritual life which connects the spirit of a living person with that of a deceased person—often called ghost. A ghost is also often understood as the apparition of a deceased person, similar in appearance to that person and encountered in places that the person frequented.

More important for this discussion is the Christian connection of spirit with personality. This is a truly novel element which we do not find in the Greek tradition, and which is also missing from Eastern conceptions of spirit. This novel conception is by no means sufficiently developed, however; for example, the idea of spirit as personality is more visible in John's Gospel than in the writings of St. Paul. Nevertheless, there are unmistakable hints of this conception of spirit as personality throughout the New Testament. Just as spirit (or soul, or matter, or reality) cannot be defined, neither can personality. Roughly speaking, personality is something which remains unchanging amidst change, the presence of the holy in the mundane. While the Greek philosophers emphasized the intellect, Christianity focuses on the heart. Instead of the Greek fascination with virtue (understood as excellence and striving toward perfection), Christianity rejects the Greek competitive element and emphasizes the relevance of suffering and compassion, as well as the miracles of grace and forgiving. Spirituality is thus understood as a benevolent energy, a God-given gift that arrives in our corporeal world from another, divine realm. Spirit is not a rationally grounded law but a state of divine inspiration.

In Augustine's philosophy, the soul is sharply separated from the body and understood as a spiritual substance (sub-stance; what stands under). Although post-medieval philosophy turns away from much in the Christian and Scholastic tradition, the founders of modern philosophy retain the idea of mental or spiritual substance. We find it, for instance, in both Descartes and Locke. Yet the development of Newton's physics—which interprets the universe not as a living organism but as a purely mechanical whole—requires a different approach to both reality and spirituality. This mechanical universe has no room for an ethical component, which can be preserved only by shifting it toward the interiority of the human person. Similarly, the universe, consisting of atoms and the forces regulating their relations in space and time, has no need—perhaps even no room—for spirits and substances. Nevertheless, the psychic and moral life of the human person must be explained somehow, and Locke persisted in defending the idea of mental substance; he built on it a conception of an indivisible human soul. Moreover, precisely this idea of an atomic and detached mental substance as the foundation of our identity served as an inspiration to the "Founding Fathers" of the young United States, who interpreted them in terms of individualism and property rights.

Despite the great success of Locke's political philosophy, his conception of substance was immediately attacked and damaged beyond repair. First Bishop Berkeley demonstrated the untenability of Locke's (and Descartes's) conception of material substance. Then Hume launched an equally devastating attack against the concept of spiritual substance. With Kant, who claimed to be awakened from his "dogmatic slumber" by Hume, the concept of substance plays a very different and far less important role. As if anticipating future developments in physics and cognitive science, Kant proposed that we think of reality in terms of functional rather than substantial concepts. This means, for example, approaching the mind not in terms of what the mind is (e.g., substance of some kind) but in terms of what the mind does; indeed, the mind is what the mind does.

After demonstrating the insurmountable boundaries of our rational knowledge of the world—for example, that we can neither prove nor disprove the existence of God, the immortality of the soul, or the possibility of freedom in the mechanically determined world—Kant shifted the emphasis from the theoretical toward practical reason. By revitalizing a Platonic dualism between how things are and how they appear to us, Kant also emphasized the gap between how things are and how they ought to be; he thereby made a Socratic shift toward free will and personal autonomy. Kant rarely used the word spirit, of course, and did not develop the Christian conception of personality at all. In Kant's philosophy, the remnants of the concept of spirit are preserved in his view of our rational capacity to act as free agents and in accordance with our conception of the moral law.

Hegel found Kant's dualisms untenable. He saw in Kant's antinomies the struggles of a great mind unable to see the historical destiny of the ever-developing spirit, leading us toward a complete realization of freedom. Central to Hegel's thought was the concept of *Geist*, which can be translated from German equally well as either "spirit" or "mind." In an exceptionally ambitious attempt at a synthesis of the Greek and the Christian traditions ever undertaken, Hegel wanted to unite intellect and will, the individual and the collective, the temporal and the eternal. He distinguished between "subjective spirit" (manifested in the thinking, feeling, and willing of an individual), "objective spirit" (which governs morality, society, and state), and "absolute spirit" (manifested in religion, art, and philosophy). Subjective spirit is a potential force, objective spirit is force in action, and absolute spirit is the aim of the force, as well as the reflection (realization) of the aim. Both nature and history are directed, in an ever-progressing dialectical movement, toward that aim, toward the Absolute. Human *Geist* is an expression of the Absolute *Geist*, through the power of which all opposites could be overcome in a higher synthesis, an ultimate monadic unity.

Hegel's grandiose conception was quickly rejected as untenable, however. As Arthur Schopenhauer argued, this synthesis is a fiction, not grounded in material reality: "Take, for example, the concept of 'spirit,' and

analyze it into its attributes: 'a thinking, willing, immaterial, simple, inde-
structible being, occupying no space.' Nothing distinct is thought in connection with it, because the elements of these concepts cannot be verified
by perceptions, for a thinking being without a brain is like digesting without a stomach."

Others, like Soren Kierkegaard, objected that Hegel "sinned" in the
opposite direction; Hegel ignored the nature of subjectivity and misunderstood the personal nature of religion.

In the next two sections, we will consider more detailed versions of these
two types of criticisms, as well as two efforts to overcome Hegel's shortcomings, through the views of Hartmann and Berdyaev.

## II. Hartmann's Conception of Spirit

One fundamental mistake of the old ontology was that it attempted to find
a single grounding principle for all reality. It tried to ground the overall
being of the world either on the principle of matter or on the principle of
spirit. Yet both views are untenable: the world is irreducible either to matter
or to spirit. Nor should we accept some version of dualism, as was com-
monly done (for example by Plato, Descartes, Locke, or Kant). Those dualisms are not sufficient to account for the complexity and richness of the
world. For that, we need a genuine pluralism, and Hartmann argued that
our world, as we know it, consists of four mutually supportive yet partially
independent layers: the inorganic, the organic, the psychic (conscious), and
the spiritual.

In our world there are beings that are purely inorganic: chairs, rocks,
and houses. There are also organic beings, like plants, but they cannot exist
without an underlying and supporting inorganic foundation. There are,
furthermore, organic and conscious beings, such as animals, whose existence would be impossible without the inorganic and organic layers. Finally,
there are human beings, who in addition to the inorganic, organic, and
conscious layers, have an element of spirituality. The layer of the spirit is
the highest, in comparison to the others, but it is also the weakest: we are
not aware of any spirit that exists without the supporting lower layers. The
material (inorganic) layer is the strongest, insofar as it provides the foundation for all others; but this layer is also the lowest.

There are numerous categories that are common to all four layers: unity and multiplicity, discretion and continuity, form and matter, identity and difference. Yet each layer also has its own defining and determining categories. For example, the categories of the corporeal world are: space and time, process and condition, substantiality and causality. The categories of the organic layers are: adaptation and purposiveness, metabolism and self-restoration, the constancy of the species and variation. In the psychic layer, the dominant categories are: act and content, consciousness and unconsciousness, pleasure and displeasure. In the realm of spirit, they are: thought, knowledge, freedom, will, evaluation, and personality. The categories that are the same for all four layers preserve the continuity of the layers. The categories that are unique to each layer enable the novel elements to emerge. Thus, reality is a dynamic whole, in constant tension, yet in constant search for balance as well.

Hartmann has a similar view on the nature of spirit. The spiritual layer is a unified layer, but in it we recognize three different manifestations of spirit. Somewhat similar to Hegel's distinction between subjective, objective, and absolute spirit, Hartmann draws the line between personal, objective, and objectified spirit. A person is that kind of being who, in every new situation, is forced to make free decisions. In addition, a person is a being who loves and hates, who can choose well or make a mistake, who has an ethos, responsibilities, and an ability to anticipate and evaluate.

Like Hegel, Hartmann believes that an objective spirit exists only in collective groups of individuals (persons), and that it represents the spirit of time; it has history, and its modifications are the historical changes we can track and explain. The "spirit of time" consists of the goals aimed at, the general tendencies and achievements, the events and the common fate of the people living at those times. It is a worldview of one group of people—of one culture and one age. This worldview is manifested in every aspect of life: language, prevailing moral values, forms of production, artistic development, and the status of sciences. Nevertheless, claims Hartmann, "in no other field of experience is the close unity and wholeness of the objective spirit as powerful and as acknowledged as in the field of religion, and the closely related mythos."

Hartmann rejects Hegel's conception of the absolute spirit. Instead, in accordance with his stratified view of reality, he speaks of the "objectified spirit," and of the manifestations of an objective spirit as captured ("objectified") in various institutions (e.g., laws) and works (say of philosophy and art) of one age. Understood in that sense, the products of an objectified spirit are both real and *irreal*. Everything that is real is temporal and individual (concrete). But the products of an objectified spirit have, besides a tangible (that is, temporal and individual aspect) also an aspect that transcends temporal limits. With regard to that aspect, they are irreal: they belong to the realm of ideas and represent what is timeless in the historical process. Yet they always need a living spirit—a person—to recognize, interpret, or simply enliven them.

Hartmann's view contains elements of both *nous* and *pneuma*. The world, for him, is a structured whole, governed by multiple categorial determinations and laws. Yet this world is by no means a fully determined and closed whole. It is a dynamic and open-ended world, without a definite goal or destination, in which the living spirit simultaneously plays a double role. On the one hand, it shapes and transforms this world; it objectifies it and gives it meaning. On the other hand, the living spirit forms and transforms itself. This *pneuma*-like quality of the spirit allows it to act both as a creative force and as a force imposing limitations on itself and the world it attempts to objectify: "in dominating nature, the spirit continues to be just as dependent upon the categories of nature as if it exercised no dominance at all, and its own categories continue to be the weaker categories. All its creative accomplishments in the realm of nature are limited by the laws of nature. Against them it can do nothing. With them it can accomplish marvels, and in this direction its only limits are those of its inventive power."

Hartmann associates this creative force primarily with our discernment and subsequent realization of values. What astonishes him is not that we have failed to make significant advancement in this direction. Far worse than lack of advancement is modern humanity's blindness to values, which he describes in terms of a narrowness of the sense of value and a lack of appreciation of the comprehensible extent of the real. For most human beings the limit of life's narrowest interests, of the most positive egoistic relations, dictated by the stress of the moment, is also the limit of their moral universe. Their spirit-less existence is a cramped, diminished life, a shriveled, distorted caricature of humanity.

We usually blame our difficulties on bad luck and unfortunate social, economic, or political circumstances. Yet, Hartmann writes, "the tragedy of man is that of one who, sitting at a well-laden table, is hungry but who will not reach out his hand, because he does not see what is before him. For the real world is inexhaustible in abundance, actual life is saturated and overflows with values, and when we lay hold of it we find it replete with wonder and grandeur."

## III. Berdyaev's View of Spirit

While Hartmann stayed closer to our common sense and common practice, Berdyaev turned against both. He demonized what he called the "objectification" of reality, which, he believed attempted to turn even spirit into a thing, an object. With the development of science in the post-medieval era, the measurable and quantifiable aspects of reality are taken as the criteria of what is real (and valuable). The whole world, including man's nature, is thus "objectified." In Berdyaev's memorable words, "Objectification is the ejection of man into the external; it is his exteriorization; it is his subjugation to the conditions of space, time, causality, and rationalization." This process includes the components of our social life as well: it leads to an unjustified glorification—Berdyaev says "sanctification"—of the state and the family, of property and society. Our ethical life becomes an adoration of such objectified and sanctified symbols, rather than a real spiritualization of living human beings.

How, then, should we understand spirit and spirituality? How should we think about the nature and destiny of the human person?

According to Berdyaev, the first steps in our spiritual reorientation must involve divorcing our understanding of spirit from materialism and from any concept of substance. Due to the many attacks on and denials of the existence of spirit, its defenders have tried to portray spirit as something objective, an object among other objects, a substance of special kind. Yet spirit is not a special kind of being—neither a different kind of object, nor a unique kind of substance. Subsequently, a philosophy of spirit should not be a philosophy of being (or ontology), but a philosophy of existence. Spirit is closer to being a subject than in it is to being an object, even though the subjectivity of spirit has to be approached carefully. Hegel and other German Idealists distorted our picture of the subject, by having no affinity toward personalism and insisting instead on an abstract person-less conception of spirit. Their concept of spirit was an abstraction, for they ranked an abstract idea higher than a concrete living being. They similarly twisted the notions of dialectic and freedom. Dialectic is essentially an "unrest of being." Hegel and his followers wanted, however, to bring this unrest to an ultimate and absolute rest (e.g., "the end of history"). And just as Hegel's dialectic led to a closure, and thereby to a denial of life, that can have no closure as long as it exists, so Hegel's freedom magically transformed itself into the iron laws of history that allow no choice and no exception.

Berdyaev's philosophy of spirit can be summarized in the following ways:

1. Spirit is concrete, personal, and subjective; as such, it is revealed only in personal existence.
2. Spirit must be understood in a personalistic way; personality is individually unique, unrepeatable, and different from the rest of the world.
3. Personal spirit is universal in terms of its content, capable of embracing the whole world by its love and cognition.
4. Personal spirit is rooted in God; it is an image of God's spirit.
5. Spirit is the breath of the divine into man.
6. Spirit is freedom; spirit cannot be determined by the world.
7. The existence of spirit does not imply or require a monistic interpretation of the world (as Hegel thought). Quite the contrary, it presupposes dualism (of a Kantian kind), or even more precisely, some kind of pluralism (in the style of Hartmann).
8. The kingdom of spirit is the realm of freedom and love.
9. Spirit is also the realm of the concrete human interiority, involving the experience of human destiny and human tragedy.
10. There are realities that belong to the different orders (physical, organic, psychic and social), but also realities like truth, goodness, beauty, value, and creative fantasy, which belong to the last order of reality, that of spirit. For example, truth is not real in the way that nature or an objective thing is, but it is real as spirit and spirituality in man's existence.
11. Spirit confirms its reality through the human person; the human person is the manifestation of spirit.
12. In the person, there is present a spiritual principle, which is transcendent in relation to the world; this spiritual principle is higher than the world.

Berdyaev found his inspiration in Christian philosophy, in the philosophy that attempts to interpret *pneuma* in a non-materialistic way. Spirit is the breath of God that permeates an individual's being and bestows on them—understood as a subject and a person—the highest value and dignity. Spirit is thus a reality that penetrates from within, from the inside, and not from the outside. Berdyaev emphasizes the fact that the human person is a subject because he stresses the relevance of act and acting: the subject is a free agent. Yet, understanding the person as subject is not just a matter of understanding them as a thinking and knowing being, because the intellect is not the central faculty of the person. The central faculty is volition, as manifested in our freedom and creativity. The human individual does not create the world, but is called to creation, called to be creative. Through a creative act, the person can not only break the limitations of egocentricity and objectivity, but can also reach out toward that which is higher than they are. Creativity is thus the foundation of humanity's relationship to God.

Creativity should not be understood in a narrow aesthetic sense, however; it deals primarily not with the formation of works of art, but with the formation of the human individual. In *The Destiny of Man* Berdyaev warned us furthermore not to try to understand creativity in any teleological sense. In his memorable words, worth citing at length, "Man's moral dignity and freedom are determined not by the purpose to which he subordinates his life but by the source from which his moral life and activity spring. It may actually be said that in a sense 'the means' which a man uses are far more important than 'the ends' which he pursues, for they express more truly what his spirit is. If a man strives for freedom by means of tyranny, for love by means of hatred, for brotherhood by means of dissension, for truth by means of falsity, his lofty aim is not likely to make our judgment of him more lenient. I actually believe that a man who worked for the cause of tyranny, hatred, falsity and dissension by means of freedom, love, truthfulness and brotherhood, would be the better man of the two. The most important thing for ethics is man's real nature, the spirit in which he acts, the presence or absence in him of inner light, of beneficent creative energy. Ethics must be based upon the conception of energy and not on the final end. It must therefore interpret freedom as the original source of action and inner creative energy and not as the power of fulfilling the law and realizing a set purpose. The moral good is not a goal but an inner force which lights up man's life from within. The important thing is the source from which activity springs and not the end toward which it is directed."

We can now see how apparently different strands of Berdyaev's philosophy of spirit intertwine. The impulse toward the objectification of the world and the sanctification of certain institutions encourages us to approach the rest of the world as our playground, as the raw material for the satisfaction of our goals and needs. In this attempt to master the world and fulfill our personal ambitions, we enslaves not only the world but ourselves as well. In pursuit of happiness, the human person loses their freedom and spiritual nature, and thus the elements of the divine within.

Berdyaev's solution is not simply to eliminate what is bad so that we can choose what is right. Our choices are either to pursue happiness without freedom, or to pursue freedom but with tragedy. While the former is obviously the choice of the majority, Berdyaev stakes human dignity on the latter: freedom with tragedy. Why is human freedom tragic, though? Why would human creativity be tragic? As stated by Berdyaev: "Man's creative act is doomed to fail within the conditions of this world. It is a tremendous effort which is destined never to succeed. Its initial impulse is to bring forth new life, to transfigure the world and usher a new heaven and a new earth; but in the conditions of the fallen world the effort turns out to be unavailing: it comes up against the inertia, the laws and compulsions of the external world, pervaded as it is by inexorable necessities."

And so we come full circle: the human individual is spirit, incarnated in a combined vehicle of soul and body. Spirit is a dynamic principle, breathed into the person by God. The person can lift their eyes up toward the divine, can spend their life pursuing creativity and freedom, but, trapped in this world and its imperfect conditions, humans seem destined to fail. And the vast majority of human beings do not even attempt to look up any more, they simply live "a life of the earth," bound to the pleasures of the flesh and disoriented about what this life and human destiny are all about. And before they can find any stable points in the labyrinth of this spirit-less, disorienting life, death sneaks in like a thief and takes away what is most valued.

What, then, is this life about? And what is so special about spirit and spirituality?

## IV. The Spirit that Enhances Life

Two mythic figures both tell the story of Western civilization, and capture its discontentedness with spirit: the figures of Prometheus and of Faust. Prometheus steals fire from the gods and brings it to people. Fire, incidentally, is one of the meanings of *pneuma*: a substance without substance, life-changing, yet also a life-endangering "thing" that allows a human being not only to cook food and get warm on a cold day, but also to forge weapons to hurt others. There is a fine line—always shifting and demanding attention—between being warmed by fire and being burned by it; finding the right distance at which to place fire has always been a challenging task. It is similar with firearms: they may be needed for protection, but often their use leads to unfortunate accidents and sometimes even horrifying massacres.

What Faust steals is not fire but knowledge. He wants to find how everything works, he searches for the underlying *logos* (*nous*) of the universe. As much as knowledge has always been desired and praised, as much as its applications (with the help of fire) have made human life so much more convenient, knowledge can also be abused, and its applications can lead to unwanted consequences. We learn not only how to build shelters, hospitals, churches, and libraries, but also how to create potent pollutants and destructive weapons. Throughout history, humans rely increasingly on their own artifacts and power-tools, rather than on what Mother Nature—or God—provides for them. And, somehow, despite the best intentions to tame Nature and put it to the service of humanity, what we produce seems in the long run to have more harmful than beneficial effects. In the process of "re-creating" creation, humans have so damaged the environment and become such efficient murderers that many now speak about the sickness and even suicidal tendencies of our civilization.

We live in a world of physical pollution, and even more spiritual pollution. Unlike chaos, which is a state of affairs (thus related to space), pollution is an event in time. Originally the word pollution referred to "a bad breath of divinity," or "blood spilled improperly or unnecessarily." The result of this pollution is disorder, or poisoning, or dirt (the antithesis of energy). Thus, pollution is a contagious affliction that calls for quarantine and cleansing. The traditional means of cleansing are water and tears of lamentation. But what if all the waters at our disposal are polluted? And are we even capable of shedding tears of lamentation?

Conceptually speaking, something has gone wrong with our spirituality. Instead of being creative and leading the way toward progressive changes, spirit got sidetracked; it got caught in a wrong conceptual net and in a wrong game. Instead of serving the forces of life, spirit is manipulated into assisting the forces of destruction. What can be done about this?

Just as we have always experienced problems with fire and knowledge, we have had a similarly ambiguous relationship with spirit; we have both welcomed it and cursed it. One of the main reasons for this is that we have always tried to capture spirit in a wrong conceptual net. Our language has perhaps obscured things more than it has helped us in the process. Our language—and thus our assertions about the world—consists essentially of nouns and verbs. Like life, spirit is too shifty, too "liquid," to be properly captured by either nouns or verbs. Like life, spirit is not a thing, not an object. Nor is it any kind of substance. What, then, is it?

If we try using verbs instead of nouns, we get caught in teleological thinking, that has been especially dominant since the development of modern science, technology, and industry. Our actions seem all to aim at something, to have a goal or purpose. Many of our actions fit this mold: they aim at something useful, at efficiency and practicality. In fact, we have become a civilization obsessed with efficiency and practicality.

As both Hartmann and Berdyaev noted, something has been obscured and missed in the process. In our goal- and result-oriented activities, we have either misunderstood or deceived ourselves about what the most important values are and whether they can be accomplished by means of our goal- and result-oriented activities. All our productivity and efficiency, all our practicality and control of nature, do not seem to help us with one crucial concern: the meaning of life. We can seemingly accomplish it all; we can produce (and consume!) more than anyone else, more than ever before. Yet, after a brief period of satisfaction, we feel empty and disoriented.

Hartmann went as far as to argue that the meaning of life depends on "useless" values. By useless he did not mean "pointless," but those that do not seem to lead to any tangible, quantifiable utilitarian benefits. One such useless value, for example, is love. Yet another is the experience of sublimity (whether in nature or in works of art). Though he did not fully explain how, such useless values have much to do with the development of both personality and spirituality.

Berdyaev tried to define spirit and spirituality in terms of a subject and a subject's acts. But that was another attempt to impose the old noun-verb categories that simply do not capture something as dynamic as spirit. In the long passage from *The Destiny of Man* that I quoted earlier, he seemed to open a new path, though without being fully aware of it or following it long enough. He said there, for instance, that "the most important thing for ethics is … the spirit in which [man] acts, the presence or absence in him of inner light, of beneficent creative energy." Focus for a moment on the phrase "the spirit in which [man] acts." This statement is neither about a noun (what action he performs), nor about a verb (what it is that he does and with what aim). Rather, it is about the way one acts, the spirit in which one acts. This is about "how" and not "what." This is about an adverb, rather than a noun or a verb. We have not sufficiently noted or developed the point Berdyaev makes here, despite the fact that it has been suggested by various ways we use the word "spirit." Something can be done in good spirit, or in bad spirit. It can be done in a spirited way, or a non-spirited way. Perhaps the key to understanding spirit is to be found, not in what is done, nor with what aim and consequences, but in what way, in what spirit, it is done.

When we do something in good spirit, this enhances life. It directs us toward higher and eternal values, toward God. And not only does it point us toward such values; we persist in that spirit even if our actions—or, more generally, our way of life—do not practically lead us to the most useful consequences or socially appreciated results. The spirit in which we act is, in a sense, inspired by God. It brings us closer to God.

This is what Berdyaev is saying, though without expressing it in these words, and perhaps without noticing the most important implications of his words: "I actually believe that a man who worked for the cause of tyranny, hatred, falsity and dissension by means of freedom, love, truthfulness and brotherhood, would be the better man of the two"—than is the one who "strives for freedom by means of tyranny, for love by means of hatred, for brotherhood by means of dissension, for truth by means of falsity." Freedom, love, truthfulness, and brotherhood are spiritual values. They are those useless values that promote and enhance life. They are values that are incompatible with killing or with the destruction of humanity.

Armed with fire and knowledge, with firearms and all-knowing iPods and computers, we claim to be working for noble goals, but the results of our actions are destroyed cities, maimed bodies, and permanently damaged souls. The results of our result-obsessed civilization are the bad breath of divinity, blood spilled improperly and unnecessarily.

It does not have to be this way. Things can change if we stop imposing our schemes on the world, stop our endless pursuit of profit, wrenching from life as many pleasures as possible. It can change if we learn to let go and trust the spirit, letting our lives be guided by that spirit we can neither completely grasp nor fully control. Hartmann and Berdyaev suspected that this road could lead us toward understanding and developing spirit in terms of personality. Though it is an ancient idea, it leads us toward an uncharted territory. We cannot anticipate what is awaiting us there, expect for one thing: the spirit we will find and develop is the spirit that kills not.

# 8. The Meaning of Life:
# Hartmann's Response to Tolstoy[1]

*In A Confession, Tolstoy describes how he, despite seeming to have every reason to be happy, had been depressed and suicidal for several years, because he could not find meaning in life. Determined either to find a definitive answer to the riddle of life's meaning or to live no longer, Tolstoy underwent a three-year-long process of soul-searching. He eventually rediscovered faith in God and became convinced that it alone could provide a solution to the riddle of life's meaning. Inspired by Hartmann, I offer a detailed analysis of this riddle and modify Tolstoy's proposed solution. Hartmann's approach opens the quest for meaning to any aspect of human experience and teaches us that this quest is not a search for some detached other-worldly transcendence. He offers a philosophy of life and consideration of life's meaning in a way that does not quench our hope or our sense of belonging in the world, but rather encourages and strengthens it. If immanence and transcendence can be integrated, they can then provide meaning for our lives.*

Hartmann's birth in 1882 coincided with the widespread circulation of Leo Tolstoy's book, *A Confession*. Tolstoy (1828–1910) was fifty-four-years old then, a wealthy man who was married with several children, and already celebrated as the author of two of the greatest novels ever written: *War and Peace* and *Anna Karenina*. In *A Confession*, Tolstoy describes how, despite seeming to have every reason to be happy, he had been depressed and suicidal for several years, because he could not find any meaning in life. He was even hiding his hunting rifles and any rope that could have tempted

---

1    A previously unpublished essay.

him to end his life. Determined either to find a definitive answer to the riddle of life's meaning or to live no longer, Tolstoy underwent a process of soul-searching. In the course of roughly three years, he systematically examined the answers that philosophy, science, and theology had traditionally offered to this riddle. While they did not satisfy him, Tolstoy rediscovered faith and became convinced that it alone could provide a solution to this terrifying riddle. He spent the remaining years of his life defending the answer he found.

While Tolstoy remained firm in his insistence on faith as the solution to the riddle of life's meaning, the circumstances surrounding the conclusion of his life call into question whether he really solved this enigma in a satisfactory way. It would seem, after all, that a man who is content and considers his life meaningful would not run away from home at the age of eighty-two, as Tolstoy did, only to die a few days later at a remote train station.

Aside from such biographical issues, there are important questions concerning Tolstoy's approach to the riddle of the meaning of life and the validity of his proposed solution: How exactly does Tolstoy present this riddle, and does it have to be approached in that way? Can faith provide a satisfactory answer to the riddle of life's meaning? And what would it take for any answer to satisfy us?

In this essay, I discuss these questions in the context of the philosophy of Hartmann and try to reconstruct the response he might have given to Tolstoy. We cannot establish with certainty whether Hartmann was familiar with Tolstoy's *A Confession*. However, we should remember that, before presenting the riddle of the meaning of life in *A Confession*, Tolstoy described it in *Anna Karenina*, completed a few years before; there, the character Levin, whom many consider to be based on Tolstoy himself, underwent a similar crisis to that which Tolstoy describes in *A Confession*. Hartmann mentions neither *Anna Karenina* nor *A Confession* in his published works. Nevertheless, considering that Hartmann spoke Russian and lived in Russia as a child and later as a student and a high school teacher, while Tolstoy was still alive and enormously popular, it would have been nearly impossible for Hartmann not to be acquainted with at least one of these two works. Whether Hartmann's thoughts about life's meaning are a response to Tolstoy's riddle or not, he offers many insights that are original and valuable.

But, before we look at Hartmann's views, we need to discuss both the manner in which Tolstoy presents the riddle and his proposed solution.

## I. Tolstoy's Riddle

In *A Confession*, Tolstoy presents a story that vividly illustrates his quandary about the meaning of life: "There is an old Eastern fable about a traveler who is taken unawares on the steppes by a ferocious wild animal. In order to escape the beast the traveler hides in an empty well, but at the bottom of the well he sees a dragon with its jaws open, ready to devour him. The poor fellow does not dare to climb out because he is afraid of being eaten by the rapacious beast, neither does he dare drop to the bottom of the well for fear of being eaten by the dragon. So he seizes hold of a branch of a bush that is growing in the crevices of the well and clings on to it. His arms grow weak and he knows that he will soon have to resign himself to the death that awaits him on either side. Yet he still clings on, and while he is holding on to the branch he looks around and sees that two mice, one black and one white, are steadily working their way round the bush he is hanging from, gnawing away at it. Sooner or later they will eat through it and the branch will snap, and he will fall into the jaws of the dragon. The traveler sees this and knows that he will inevitably perish. But while he is still hanging there, he sees some drops of honey on the leaves of the bush, stretches out his tongue and licks them. In the same way I am clinging to the tree of life, knowing full well that the dragon of death inevitably awaits me, ready to tear me to pieces, and I cannot understand how I have fallen into this torment. And I try licking the honey that once consoled me, but it no longer gives me pleasure. The white mouse and the black mouse—day and night—are gnawing at the branch from which I am hanging. I can see the dragon clearly and the honey no longer tastes sweet. I can see only one thing; the inescapable dragon and the mice, and I cannot tear my eyes away from them. And this is no fable but the truth, the truth that is irrefutable and intelligible to everyone.

What a story! What an approach to life! Perhaps only Augustine and Calvin, or Hobbes and Schopenhauer, could regard life in such a pessimistic way.

114

After years of searching, Tolstoy believed he could provide a definitive and universal answer to this riddle: "Whichever way I put the question: How am I to live? the answer is always: according to God's law. Or to the question: is there anything real that will come of my life? the answer is: eternal torment or eternal bliss. Or, to the question: What meaning is there that is not destroyed by death? the answer is: unity with the infinite, God, heaven."

Let us offer some preliminary comments on the way Tolstoy presents the riddle and on his proposed solution.

1. In the sections of *A Confession* preceding the fable, Tolstoy presents the puzzle of life's meaning in a manner reminiscent to the quandary of Faust: "either I will come to know the meaning of life, or I will not live." The scenario presented in the fable, however, is much darker, virtually apocalyptic: it is precisely because I know what the world is like and because I am aware of the inevitability of death, that I realize life is meaningless and that all my hopes are doomed. The awareness of my helplessness in the face of death makes my life pointless.

It is possible to say that Tolstoy's fable is exaggerated or, more precisely, that it relies on a "distortion for the sake of truth." This, however, is the precise and proper function of fables in general: by exaggerating their subjects, they highlight their truth. In a sense, fables function in a manner similar to caricatures, which deliberately overemphasize certain features of the face in order to reveal, by means of exaggeration, the person's essential characteristics.

2. What is problematic about Tolstoy's fable is not that it exaggerates and distorts. To see where the real problem lies, we must observe that neither in the fable itself nor in his proclaimed answer does Tolstoy mention our relations with other human beings. They do not seem to exist, or our relation to them does not seem to be of importance in any way. Tolstoy presents the individual as not merely powerless and helpless but as isolated and lonely as well. We could even say that Tolstoy really presents an analogon of a living individual: a solitary creature whose anxiety overwhelms them completely, rather than a concrete human being, with multiple gifts and different sides to their personality. Would not a living human have something God-like in them? Would this person have no significant accomplishments and no legitimate hopes?

3. Just as the fable is devoid of reference to either society or history, so too is it devoid of respect for the real, concrete world. Tolstoy presents the fable and offers an answer to its query as if we lived surrounded exclusively by the hostile forces of nature. Notice furthermore that the riddle never mentions God. Tolstoy does not explain why, if God exists, He created such a riddle for us, or what God may want of us, or how He could help us.

4. Tolstoy's fable also does not mention any truly significant and lasting experience of goodness, beauty, or the joys of life. He merely notes that there are "two drops of honey" that once made his life sweet. In the sections of *A Confession* following the fable, he identifies these "sources of consolation" as his family and his writings. Can we expect from life nothing more than a small consolation for our unavoidable death? Can such consolation provide a solution to the riddle of life's meaning?

What is particularly surprising is that Tolstoy does not consider the following possibilities: If the two drops of honey no longer taste sweet, and if the inevitability of our death is the only truth and "all the rest is a lie," how can his faith in God avert that awful destiny awaiting him? How can his life possibly gain meaning through faith, when it seems that whether one has faith or not, whether God exists or not, alters no fact about life itself. So, is faith in God also a lie?

5. Faith may, indeed, be a response to the arbitrariness of life. Nevertheless, faith is not necessarily a denial of this arbitrariness, nor its resolution, but simply a response. But what kind of a response is it, and in what sense may it be called an adequate response? Is this response sufficient to answer the riddle of life's meaning? If not, what else must be added? Similarly, we need to realize that, although the sheer fact of the existence of God may hold some promise of an answer to the question of life's meaning, it does not by itself guarantee anything. It does not even guarantee that life has any meaning. Nor need one have any conception of God, to accept the idea that life may have meaning.

6. The most important question in this context seems to be: If we have faith in God, how does this change anything, when that faith seems neither necessary nor sufficient for solving the riddle of life's meaning? In *A Confession*, Tolstoy offers two types of replies. In one, he is either vague or elusive, and claims more than he seems entitled to. In the other, Tolstoy is

more specific, yet still one wonders why he could not offer the same answer without relying on religion, faith, and God.

Here is an example of the first, vague type of answer: "'Live in search of God and there will be no life without God!' And more powerfully than ever before everything within and around me came to light, and the light has not deserted me since. And I was saved from suicide."

Tolstoy's second type of reply is more specific: "I returned to the idea that the single most important aim of my life is to improve myself, that is, to live according to this will ... In other words I returned to a belief in God, in moral perfection, and to that tradition which had given life a meaning." At the end of this chapter, namely Chapter 12 of *A Confession*, and while still pursuing the same line of reasoning, Tolstoy concludes: "The shore was God, the direction was tradition, and the oars were the freedom given to me to row towards the shore and unite with God. In this way the force of life rose up within me and I started to live once again." Tolstoy does not discuss the possibility that our moral improvement is possible without faith in God, or even that our faith need not have a divine being as its object.

7. Tolstoy presents the challenge of finding life's meaning in terms of our smallness and limitations, our finitude and imperfection. To overcome such obstacles, he believes that we must turn to the infinite and perfect: to God and His alleged Law. Without faith in God, he insists, it is impossible to live: "To know God and to live are one and the same thing. God is life." Tolstoy offers no clarification about how these two are so intimately related, nor about why they ought to be. Moreover, he insists that in order to live according to God one must renounce all the comforts of life; one must work, be humble, suffer, and be merciful. It looks again as if the question of life's meaning has merely one dimension: the vertical, which takes into account only man's relationship to God. The horizontal dimension, that of our bonds and interactions with other human beings—and with the rest of the world—he completely ignores. Paradoxically, Tolstoy recommends a life of monastic self-denial of our life-impulses as the only way to reach life's meaning. Even more boldly, he asserts that denial of the concrete, this-worldly existence is the one way to make life meaningful—but what in life is even left to be meaningful if what we recognize as life is so repressed?

8. The difference in perspective that faith in God permits now emerges a bit more clearly, although Tolstoy's view is neither fully supported nor sufficiently convincing. He argues that worldly values, such as family, fame, and other pleasures, are insufficient to give life meaning, supposedly because they are all "temporary" and "finite"; at the end of life, as Tolstoy sees it, death turns the edifice built on such values into ashes and dust. Tolstoy believes that the answer to the question of life's meaning lies in our uniting "with the infinite, God, heaven." Can this faith in the invisible reverse the arbitrariness and the pointlessness that, for Tolstoy, characterizes this life? Or can it only offer a "rescue" for us after death, perhaps in the form of the "Kingdom of God"? While this Kingdom may or may not come, Tolstoy does not address the question which seems most significant for our consideration of the riddle of *life's* meaning: Does the prospect of inevitable death prevent our lives from being meaningful *while they last*?

## II. Hartmann's Approach to the Riddle of Meaning

Tolstoy was not a nihilist. Just as Descartes wanted to refute skepticism by introducing the most radical doubt, Tolstoy presented an apocalyptic story in order to refute it and establish a definitive answer to the riddle of life's meaning. But, just as Descartes was considered by his contemporaries to be a "*sceptique malgré lui*," Tolstoy's appeal to God as well as to our faith in a divine being sounded equally hollow in the ears of his Western readers. Nietzsche's proclamation that God is dead, which occurred at roughly the same time as Tolstoy's attempt to renew faith, impressed his contemporaries far more. It pushed Western civilization, which was then losing hope in material and social progress, further toward nihilism. This additional relativization and subjectification of all values found powerful expression in literature, in the works of Kafka and Camus, and in philosophy and religion, in the works of the existentialists. Despite Tolstoy's insistence, the bond between humanity and God appeared, in his time, to have been broken beyond repair. Humanity was left to feel homeless in a hostile, arbitrary, and even absurd world. Not the prospect of death, but life itself, seems to have become the source of humanity's greatest terror.

Like Tolstoy, and unlike Kafka, Camus, and their followers, Hartmann believed in the possibility of a positive resolution to the riddle of life's meaning.

Unlike Tolstoy, who staked everything on man's vertical relationship with God, Hartmann suggested that we first move in a horizontal direction. Instead of looking for an escape from the finite into the infinite, Hartmann believed we must immerse ourselves in the finite, while the infinite—not in the form of God, but in the form of ideal being—may still play an important role in the answer to the riddle. Instead of seeking the infinite and the absolute, we should try to understand how we are grounded in the concrete and temporal world. While there is no denying that life is cruel and arbitrary, concerning itself with humanity no more than it concerns itself with the earthworm, this is not all that life is. Similarly, while there can be no denying our limitations and imperfections—no denying that each of us is little more than a speck of dust in an infinite universe—this is not all we are, either. Life is not as confusing and pointless as Tolstoy's fable indicates, nor is the human person as helpless and powerless as Kafka and Camus presume. The human individual, although limited in many ways, can nevertheless be free, creative, responsive, and accountable. A human is not simply a lonely, homeless individual but can be, or at least become, a fully developed person.

Hartmann's central idea is that, for life to have meaning, that meaning can be found only through our personal participation in the fullness of this limited and imperfect life. Only such participation can make us receptive to what is significant as well as open to whatever has value and meaning. Our cosmic insignificance and transitoriness do not impair our capacity to have meaningful lives. The human is not just a passive object in the world, a defenseless and helpless plaything of the titanic forces of nature, as Tolstoy's fable would have it.

While Tolstoy is seeking a definitive meaning of life—expecting that life must be "either eternal torment or eternal bliss"—Hartmann focuses on any meaning and recognizes that life may be both torment and bliss—just not eternally one or the other. The human individual bestows meaning insofar as one is capable of mediating between the real and the ideal. For Tolstoy, values are either "earthly" insofar as they are temporary and relative, or they are "heavenly," insofar as they are eternal and unchangeable, and presented in the form of "God's Law." Hartmann's view indicates a further contrast between his approach and that of Tolstoy. While Tolstoy does not speak of values in connection with our search for meaning (besides the two drops of honey), Hartmann's insistence on values adds a dimension, missing

119

in Tolstoy's fable, that is indispensable for the consideration of life's meaning. The very word "meaning" directs us toward what is significant and valuable. It directs us toward values, which for Hartmann are in the realm of ideal being. Meaning should not be regarded as a kind blanket that can be thrown over the world. We can agree with Tolstoy that the world is not oriented toward humanity. This does not mean, however, that the human person cannot be oriented toward the world.

Tolstoy's unfortunate avoidance of any further discussion of values seems to preclude the possibility that humans can orient themselves toward the world. We should recognize that the way Tolstoy's fable presents the phenomenon of human participation in the world is too narrow. As described in the fable, our participation in the world is only directed toward self-preservation, and toward the realization of practical values of immediate concern. Hartmann's insight is that such narrowness is not only unnecessary but also leads to moral poverty and a perception of life as empty and lacking, which in turn leads us to question whether life has any meaning. By focusing only on tasks of immediate practical significance, we become blind to the spiritual values and riches of real life. In Hartmann's rendering of Tolstoy's query, the tragedy of humanity is not that we cannot avoid death. The true tragedy occurs when a person is alive but spiritually dead due to their way of living and their blindness.

Fortunately, it is possible to learn to see the world as it is, to wake up and train our capacity to differentiate values. Such awakening and training engage us simultaneously in the participation in the fullness of life and in the realization of our own human potential. And the prerequisite for such a reorientation is neither fear of death nor anxiety over our existence, but a loving gaze directed toward the world. Our search for the meaning of life presupposes a sensitive and appreciative look at everything of value with which we get in touch. This being the case, both Tolstoy's approach to the riddle of life's meaning, and the typical human approach to that riddle, are based on the same mistake. According to Hartmann, "To pass a human being by unnoticed, to pass a community by, to brush past a historical crisis of the world—in all this appears the same aspect of the same ethos, the same going empty away, the same self-condemnation and self-annihilation. It is the same blindness to values and the same squandering of them. Only once it is given to a generation what returns neither to it nor to any other;

as only once to an individual it is given the one-time fullness of the moment. And it is the same sin against the meaning of life, against the metaphysical significance of human existence—the same absurdity."

We must relearn how to look at the world lovingly and with a sense of wonder. Despite all the threatening and overwhelming forces of the world, and despite the terrible events that wound our humanity and shake our confidence in life's meaning, we must find a new devotion for what is great in life, both as a whole, and in its minutest parts. If we can reorient ourselves in this way, we will realize not only that life can have meaning but also that there are endless acts that bestow this meaning on our lives.

## III. Bestowing Meaning

The idea that there are endless acts that can bestow meaning is crucially significant to Hartmann. The keys to understanding it are the words "bestowing" and "acts." To bestow something means to confer or to present, to give or to convey to another—whether it be an honor, right, or gift. The word "bestow" is normally used in cases of giving something of great value or importance. Furthermore, bestowing presupposes that what is being given is not already there in one's possession, or inherent in one's being.

Hartmann does not believe that the world as such has meaning. It simply is, and for the most part it is indifferent to meaning. What is important is that the world is not opposed to meaning or hostile to it. If it were, the idea of bestowing meaning would itself be meaningless.

This clarification does not turn the question of meaning into an easy problem to solve. Hartmann readily admits that the riddle of meaning is one of those metaphysical problems that is essentially unsolvable—at least, if we are speaking of the problem of the meaning of the world as a whole and human life as a whole. In *Aesthetics*, Chapter 35, sections a and b, where Hartmann discusses the problem of meaning in the most detailed way in his entire opus, he begins with a curious remark: "So long as there was a belief in a higher power, the question [of life's meaning] does not arise, because it has already been answered through faith." He does not explain why, however, and we will return to the topic of the relevance of faith for the question of meaning later, in section VI. Hartmann adds that, if faith collapses—as he presumably believes happened on a massive scale with the advancement of modernity, especially in the nineteenth century—then the issue of meaning becomes a serious problem: "for who would want to, or be able to, live a life that has no sense?"

As a preliminary consideration, Hartmann criticizes the Platonic approach to the problem of meaning. His criticism is really directed toward two principles, which are inherent not only to the Platonic but also to every teleological approach to the problem of meaning: that the world itself should be understood via an analogy with humanity, as guided by an understanding and purposive consciousness; and that humanity's future goals must be posited and the means for their realization be chosen antecedent to those goals. The failure of teleological approaches to the problem of meaning lies in their unacceptable anthropomorphism. Such anthropomorphism is usually hidden, but once it is unveiled, this has fatal implications not only for the Platonic theory of Forms, but also for any other theologized version of the teleological approach to the world and human life. Hartmann believes that neither the meaning of the world nor the meaning of human life can be based on teleology. They also cannot be based on theology, as Tolstoy believed.

Our traditional way of thinking about meaning has also been misguided due to two more principles, both of which, Hartmann argues, we should reject. The first is the belief that meaning can lie only in the origins of things, and cannot enter the world subsequently; the second is that meaning can inhere only in the whole of the world, from which it extends to all of its parts, human lives included.

Such mistaken principles have been adopted because, traditionally, our metaphysical thinking has been obsessively oriented toward the search for general and universal principles—even where there are none. Oriented toward such principles, metaphysical thinking ignored the things closest to humanity, the things intertwined with human life in its concreteness as manifested in the acts and activities of living human beings. Once we free ourselves from these anthropomorphic and theological prejudices and approach the riddle of meaning from an opposite angle, we realize that "there are endless things in life, which, though limited and individual, are meaningful without recourse to principles or to a greater whole." As he elaborates, every morally good act, every wise thought, every adequate response to a value, is meaningful and bestows additional meaning simply by occurring:

"Out of itself alone: that means that it does not have meaning only for the sake of something else. Such is every act of benevolence, every participation in the spiritual and the inner life—every sympathetic understanding and every interpersonal involvement that breaks through icy loneliness precisely where a person wishes to be seen and appreciated—are meaningful for themselves alone; yet they bestow a meaning upon other things, and a deep need of the human heart for the realization of meaning is thereby satisfied."

How simple, yet profound! Change the angle at which one looks at the problem, and it does not disappear, as in Wittgenstein, but rather appears in an entirely new light. Just as in our feelings for values we recognize when something touches our lives, so too do we instantly recognize here what has been missing, what has been overlooked—even though it has always been right in front of us. If the world had a predetermined meaning, for which the metaphysical thinkers of the past have searched in vain, what would be the function and role of the human person in that world? The person would be little more than a puppet, or a slave, of the higher powers that have prearranged the world. Hartmann's approach restores the dignity of the human person without denying our smallness and limitations. Although imperfect and impotent in the face of the titanic forces of nature, the person, even with limited powers, is capable of bestowing meaning and value upon the world and their own unique place in it, by means of their feeling for values, and ability to realize values.

The human person is a creature with the power to bestow meaning. Meaning is not something that is already there, planted in the world from its beginnings. Rather, meaning is brought about through humanity's interaction with the world when the individual employs the gifts of their own nature. Among such gifts, Hartmann emphasizes the following: the power of self-determination, the gift of freedom and decision-making, the capacity to anticipate ("man's providence"), the capacity to posit ends for actions, the consciousness of values and the ability to distinguish good and evil, and the gift of sympathetic understanding and appraisal of everything that one encounters.

We can now identify, using Hartmann's ideas, what is fundamentally missing in Tolstoy's fable: namely, the recognition of the human person's ability to relate to the world in all its aspects rather than being focused merely on one's own powerlessness within the world, and the inevitable approach of death. Tolstoy forgets, or ignores, the capacity of the human person that he, Tolstoy, had in such a great degree: the creative capacity. This ability is not manifested in the kind of majestic projects and undertakings that seem appropriate for divine beings and superhumans, for humans do not have such vast abilities. But the human person has an ability to create on a small scale, and through such creative acts, one can bestow meaning upon the world and one's own life in it.

## IV. Aesthetic Values and Life's Meaning

A primary reason why Hartmann discusses the question of life's meaning in *Aesthetics* is that certain aesthetic gifts render the human person capable of bestowing meaning. Our capacity to create goes hand in hand with our ability to see, and that the gift of seeing the world as something beautiful is as important for our capacity to bestow meaning as our moral gifts are. All meaning is connected with values, and all values are important for meaning, including the lower values (such as vital values). Hartmann believes in the existence of higher values—which he calls "spiritual" and among which he counts cognitive, ethical, and aesthetic values—and he argues that these values play a special role in bestowing meaning. This "value triangle" reminds us of the old Platonic triangle of the True, the Good, and the Beautiful. Yet unlike Plato, Hartmann sharply separates the axiological and ontological aspects of these values. Ontologically, values are not the most real of all beings, as in Plato's philosophy, but rather have a kind of existence in the realm of the ideal. Nor does Hartmann say much about the relevance of cognitive values for the meaning of life, despite indicating that they should not be forgotten or underestimated. As is to be expected, his discussion of life's meaning is most directly related to moral values. Where Hartmann surprises us, and makes a unique contribution to the subject, is in his explanation of the relation of aesthetic values to the meaning of life.

Aesthetic values deal with issues that are "less urgent" than those pertaining to moral questions. While moral values are tied to such issues and are "heavy," aesthetic values are "light" and detached from the gravity of moral considerations. Precisely because of that detachment—or the "disinterested interest," as Kant calls it—they represent especially pure forces in the bestowal of meaning. The joy we feel while standing in the presence of something of absolute intrinsic value can inspire an awareness that life is worth living. The joy taken in an object with such a value and the pleasure we gain from living in a world where such wonderful things exist allow us to experience both the world and our lives as full of meaning, regardless of what else is happening in that same world. This is why our experience of the bestowal of meaning is stronger and purer in our encounter with aesthetic values than in our encounter with moral values. While Hartmann also ties this bestowal to an artist's creative ability, he reminds us that a viewer must be creative to a significant degree as well: "The viewer, too, carries the same bestowal of meaning to his part in life. To be able to 'see' what is beautiful does much: without the viewer, there is no beauty, and to be sure, he must be a viewer in a specific way ... Accordingly, the man who beholds and grasps values is there also with the creator."

While Tolstoy insists that we must learn life's meaning by purifying, restraining, and detaching ourselves from all lower, material and body-related values, Hartmann goes in a different direction and connects meaning with a gift: "What is the highest value in life has something of the character of giving gifts." Hartmann borrows this idea from Nietzsche's discussion of the bestowing virtue (*schenkende Tugend*) in *Thus Spoke Zarathustra*. Hartmann then seems to turn more in the direction of Tolstoy than of Nietzsche when he compares the bestowing of virtue with a gift: the experience of seeing the world as beautiful makes us feel as if we have received a gift from heaven; it is a feeling comparable to what religious people describe as a sense of grace. The gift that we receive feels like a miracle: unearned and useless yet received with joy and appreciation.

The connection with Nietzsche is more obvious when the act of bestowing virtue is compared to the radiance of gold. The experience of beauty, whether in nature or in any work of art, sheds radiance on human life, a life which is too often one of compromises, half-measures, and endless anxieties. Precisely in such a life, insists Hartmann, the bestowal is stronger and more meaningful: "Just therein is reflected the bestowal of meaning, which emanates from beauty ... such that this radiance penetrates the darkness of suffering and distress—it enters those places where other powers have lost their strength to succor us."

At this point, Hartmann introduces three more insights; they are his most important contribution to our discussion of the meaning of life. The first deals with the change that is introduced through the bestowal of meaning, the second with the significance of the ideal (and thus of values in general), and the third with our reception of such gifts.

To clarify the first insight, recall Tolstoy's fable again: our position in the world is helpless. No matter what we try, the forces that act upon us are overwhelming and our death is inevitable. Hartmann's first insight is that what changes through the bestowal of gifts such as beauty is not the external circumstances. Such gifts modify only our inner psychic orientation: "nothing is removed, yet a spiritual good is bestowed, things imponderable and immeasurable are given to us for our own. The power that expresses itself here is not real, but it is a power that grasps, validates, and justifies our real living heart, a power that extends as far as our philosophical picture of the world."

Would this be enough to satisfy Tolstoy? Would it change anything for the man who is hanging on the narrow branch above the abyss and will soon fall in? Hartmann's second insight addresses this issue, at least partially. While moral values seem to have a more direct impact on our lives, aesthetic values have only an indirect one. But the indirectness of that impact does not make it less important. The experience of beauty detaches us from our daily worries and the obligations that weight upon us. But that which appears to have been lifted out of the bounds of this life makes a curious reentry. It reenters our lives not to be fully assimilated into them in any direct practical sense, but rather to guide us and inspire us through its radiance. Enjoying the gift of beauty is not an escape from life and its burdens and limitations. It is rather a temporary distancing from life, which enables us to see it from a different perspective and thus make an impact on everything that happens "on the surface of life."

This topic is of such importance to Hartmann that he returns to it in the very last paragraph of his *Aesthetics*. The power to enlighten and to convince, in places where no demonstration could ever convince anyone, is a purely spiritual one. It is the power to direct the gaze upon that which should be beheld, and to bring about the act of conversion. "For that is decisive. And just for that reason, so much in human life depends upon our living, alongside of all actuality, a 'life in the Idea.' We can do that because we possess the power of aesthetic beholding."

This "life in the Idea" can make sense only if we remember that, for a thing to be a gift, two persons are needed: the giver and the receiver. Similarly, the purely aesthetic realm requires a creator and a spectator. The idea that giving takes two can be expanded to other areas of human experience, as well. Especially, it can be applied to that area on which Tolstoy's fable is the weakest: our relationship to others. We should then combine this reminder with another one, which Hartmann expresses explicitly in the introduction to *Ethics*: in order to participate in the fullness of life, we must approach the world with a loving gaze and a loving attitude. Keeping these insights in mind, we should not be surprised by the concluding paragraph of Hartmann's discussion of personal love: "Thus personal love, bestowing virtue, gives an ultimate meaning to life; it is already fulfilment in germ, an uttermost value of selfhood, a bestowal of import upon human existence—useless, like every genuine self-subsistent value, but a splendor shed upon our path."

This is what participation in the fullness of life and appreciation of its riches amounts to: to be human is to be the mediator between the realms of real and ideal being. Such a mediator is neither a passive observer of the world, nor a mere beholder of the values that are bestowed, in their ideal nature, upon humans. Genuine mediation requires not only the feeling and discernment of values, but also human attempts at the realization of values. Such realization is indeed possible in the real world and in our relations with other human beings. For Hartmann, the most fulfilling of these relations is that of love. In his view, the love felt by two human beings for each other is, more than anything else, conducive to the bestowal of meaning in life.

## V. Faith and Life's Meaning

Although Tolstoy does not understand faith as creed, faith for him is nevertheless faith in God. And since, for Tolstoy, God is not a person, he speaks of faith in terms of our relationship with the infinite. Perhaps intuiting that this may not be enough to answer the riddle of life's meaning, Tolstoy adds to his argument with the explanation that faith is a conscious relationship with the infinite, from which we derive guidance on how to live our lives meaningfully. And he stresses even more strongly: "Faith is a knowledge of the meaning of life, the consequence of which is that man does not kill himself but lives. Faith is the force of life ... Without faith it is impossible to live."

Hartmann is not a believer in any traditional sense, but he shares with Tolstoy a conviction that faith is of high value. For him, faith is a kind of foundation, and without faith it is hardly possible to live the life of a human being. Nevertheless Hartmann's view of faith is fundamentally different from Tolstoy's. First, it is not a faith in God or any supernatural or divine being. It is more of a faith in the general structure and orderliness of the world. Second, and more related to our topic, it is a faith in the great ideals, as well as a faith that there is something good in every human being.

For Tolstoy, faith is not about creed; it is about certainty. It provides him with a sense of assurance strong enough to allow him to overcome— or at the very least neutralize—his fear of death and his anxiety about the apparent meaninglessness of life. In a comment directed against Heidegger (and the existentialist's approach to life in general), Hartmann argues that fear and anxiety are the worst possible grounds for any philosophical reflection about the meaning of life: "The person filled with dread is such that he is incapable of achieving a sober vision of life and what is, in the way that it is." Nor should faith be identified with knowledge of any definitive rational kind. Faith is not knowledge of the meaning of life, but it serves to evoke that meaning and point us in the right direction: "So long as a man retains a spark of moral feeling, the impulse lives in him, not to fall short of what is expected of him. This is a well-known method of moral discipline; but that there is in faith a general power of awaking the moral life, has been less widely recognized; yet it deserves to become a common possession. Finally, there is something good in everyone. And it grows with the exercise of it and through encouragement. It languishes through lack of appreciation. Faith can transform a man, toward good or evil, according to what he believes. This is its secret, its power to remove mountains."

Adjacent to Hartmann's claim that there is something good in everyone is his recognition that not all is good in any one of us, nor in life in general. Faith is not a blanket-like belief to be thrown over the world to veil its complexity. Quite the opposite: faith demands of us a discriminatory judgement. Faith is not a knowledge that can be possessed once and for all, but rather something that is obtained by striving, and a fruit of moral ripeness.

Following this line of thought, Hartmann connects faith not with knowledge but with wisdom. The Greek word *sophia* is rendered in Latin as *sapientia*, which should not be interpreted in any intellectualistic or moralistic way. The original meaning of *sapientia* is "moral taste," which is a capacity directed toward fullness of life and an affirming attitude toward whatever is of value. Wisdom, then, is "ethical spirituality, the attitude of the ethos as the ultimate spiritual factor in humanity, dominating the whole life."

The wise person carries into all their relationships the standards of value which they possess in their spiritual "taste," and their entire outlook on life is saturated with these standards. This primacy of spiritual values does not come to us through knowledge of the divine commandments or by way of reflection. It occurs as an immediate, intuitive, emotionally-toned divination, which derives from the center of moral perception and penetrates all our experiences.

Instead of being dependent upon God and our relationship with the infinite, our quest for meaning ought to be directed toward other humans: toward concrete and finite, fallible and living individuals. The quest for meaning is not an intellectual query. It is the concrete struggle of the human being to develop their own personality and establish an open-minded, sensitive, appreciative. and loving relationship with other real human beings and with the virtually inexhaustible complexity and richness of the real world. Faith is not a matter of God's revelation but a revelation of the creative power in humanity. It is not a power that binds humanity to God but rather a power that binds one human being to others, and to the rest of the world, as part of a devotion to the highest purposes of which humanity is capable. Human life is meaningful insofar as we can behold and participate in the world, in all its depth and richness. Although such an orientation is directed toward the highest ideals and values, this does not mean it is specifically directed toward God, or dependent on any divine being. It depends, instead, on our attention and responsiveness, and finds its highest fulfilment in our loving relations with both other human beings, and with the world in all its concrete manifestations.

In opposition to Tolstoy's "oriental" fable, Hartmann's account takes a "Western" turn. Not only is personality different from one individual to the next; this difference is as it should be. Precisely through such differences, a person is unique and irreplaceable: "The specific direction of his nature actually exists only once, and only in him. In him it co-exists with the universal direction of human nature. In him the individual ethos entrenches itself upon the universal ethos."

Not every personality is equally developed, nor is everyone equally capable of bestowing meaning. Nevertheless, whoever has truly developed their personality carries their standards with them, beyond all doubts; in following these standards, one is loyal to oneself. Such a person shows definite and unmistakable sympathies and antipathies, for which they may be able to give no account other than that this is what they must, of necessity, feel. This person sees the world in as no one else sees it, in a light of their own—the light of their preferred values, while living in accordance with those values. The human individual is, in a sense, a world unto themself, and the meaning the person bestows is uniquely their own.

## VI. Faith in Man and Faith in God

Tolstoy's quest for meaning was motivated by fears and anxieties that ultimately overpowered him: What is going to happen to me? If I am going to die anyway, then why live? How could life possibly have any meaning when death is inevitable?

Hartmann's reply to Tolstoy's questions can be summed up in the following points.

(i) Let us redirect our attention back to reality. Nietzsche's proclamation of the death of God is not a disaster, but an opportunity to turn our gaze back to the world and search for our place and role in that world with fresh eyes. By paying attention to the concrete and real world, we discover what is valuable in the world, and what is best in us. So, Hartmann's message to Tolstoy might be: you did not look closely enough; you did not take a long enough look at the world. Had you done so, you would see more than just what is terrible in it, and would not feel so compelled to search for salvation outside the world itself.

(ii) One thing we discover when we redirect our attention to the real world is that we are not trapped in that world, as Tolstoy's fable indicates. Nor is the world a place that contains only beasts that chase us or dragons that await to devour us. As there are "bad" dragons and beasts, there are good ones as well, which we must discover and whose protection we need to find. Moreover, instead of thinking about how death awaits us, we should enjoy life as a journey, regardless of its ultimate destination.

(iii) When we approach Tolstoy's questions in this spirit, we realize that Hartmann redirects them away from a discussion of the meaning of life, and toward the theme of life's worth: Is life worth living? If so, what gives it this worth? A short answer is that life can be worth living if we learn how to lovingly embrace that life and enhance our own capacities and gifts in the process. Instead of a primarily cognitive attitude, we should assume one that is fundamentally value-oriented and, in the broader sense of the word, erotic. Eros in this sense is that force that connects us to the real world and to other human beings in it, transforming us in the process. Instead of being helpless, powerless, homeless, and lost in the world, the world becomes our home and shelter, in the fullest sense.

(iv) The process of our loving interaction with the world requires a shift in our search for meaning from an ego-centric to an ex-centric orientation. The human person must be orientated toward the world; only through this outward orientation can one figure out their own place and role in reality. Instead of passively waiting for whatever is going to happen to us next, we should redirect our attention to the active powers in humanity. The key to the meaning of life is to be found in the way we respond to the world and participate in the course of events.

(v) For Tolstoy, the quest for meaning is a religious one. While Hartmann defends an essentially humanistic, rather than theistic answer to the quest for meaning, it could be argued that he radicalizes Tolstoy's approach: the quest for meaning becomes a spiritual quest, focusing primarily (although not exclusively) on spiritual values. One disadvantage of a narrower, exclusively religious solution to the riddle of meaning is that it not only places the human person in a passive position, but also insists on one blanket solution no matter for every situation, and every human being. Such a solution ignores not only the richness and complexity of the world, but also the uniqueness and gifts of each individual. It neglects the truth that the answer to the riddle of meaning has to be "earned" by each one of us, through our way of life; due to our unique personalities, the answer is at least slightly different for every person, and even will vary throughout the course of a single life.

(vi) The religious solution has a few other disadvantages worth mentioning. For one thing, it treats creation only as an act of God, which is completed once and for all. Hartmann's approach not only focuses on human creativity, but also calls our attention to a need for a continuous creation and recreation of ourselves and our relationship with the world. There is no limit to the number of acts capable of bestowing meaning, and the process of bestowing meaning never ends.

(vii) A religious solution is oriented almost exclusively toward the narrowly conceived moral aspect of human life. Hartmann's approach opens up the quest for meaning to any aspect of human experience, including the whole spectrum of our spiritual values. Beauty is as significant in the quest for meaning as goodness is, and love may be even more fundamentally relevant than either beauty or goodness. For not only does loving other human beings bestow the highest meaning upon life, but a loving attitude toward reality is a prerequisite for any kind of meaningful experience.

(viii) The quest for life's meaning is not a search for a form of consolation. Life is full of conflicts, as it involves promises, betrayals, disappointments, and achievements. Fluid and ever shifting as it is, life offers no guarantees. Moreover, life continually reminds us of the inevitability of death. We need a philosophy of life and a consideration of life's meaning that does not shut off our hope or our sense of belonging in the world, but rather encourages and strengthens it. Tolstoy raises the question: "How could life possibly have any meaning when death is inevitably approaching?" Hartmann answers with a question of his own: How could life not have meaning when we direct a loving gaze toward the world and are able to perceive it, and ourselves in it, with all its limitations and imperfections, all its wonders and treasures, unexhausted and inexhaustible?

## VII. Life Full of Meaning

At the time Hartmann died—in 1950—humanity was in great distress. The scars left by the Second World War had yet to heal, and the world's most powerful nations had already begun their nuclear arms race, fueled by a maddening and delusional hatred as well as a sense of self-righteousness. The two World Wars and the newly unfolding "Cold War" were demoralizing enough to undermine any realistic belief in progress, humanism, science, or any political system. Both Tolstoy's faith in God and Hartmann's faith in humanity would seem to have been squarely defeated. The existentialists Kafka and Camus spoke far more to a wounded and disoriented humanity than any optimistic voice from the past could. Nihilism and subjectivism seemed the most credible "wisdom." And the subsequent rapid development of technology added more confusion, while shifting our focus toward another possible "solution" to the question of life's meaning. And now, seventy years after Hartmann's death, it might seem futile to search for any higher value, goal, or being to which we could dedicate our lives; rather, we should resign ourselves to dwelling in a virtual reality. To many, the riddle of life's meaning seems to have no solution beyond the prospect of escape from reality, escape from real life.

While Kafka's character Josef K. could not find a passage back toward human beings and the real world, we now willingly build walls of separation. Camus' character Meursault survived by making himself numb, but Camus himself could not do it. Five years before he died—and five years after Hartmann died—Camus published an essay with the title "Helen's Exile." Alarmed by the horrifying hubris of humanity, Camus thought we should slow down, recall our roots, and heed the wisdom of the Greeks: "We have exiled beauty; the Greeks took up arms for her. First difference, but one that has a history. Greek thought always took refuge behind the conception of limits. It never carried anything to extremes, neither the sacred nor reason, because it negated nothing, neither the sacred nor reason. It took everything into consideration, balancing shadow with light. Our Europe, on the other hand, off in the pursuit of totality, is the child of disproportion. She negates beauty, as she negates whatever she does not glorify."

I doubt that it is possible for us to return to these ideals of the ancient Greeks, but we can still learn some lessons from them. Beauty should not be negated, and Hartmann realized this fact perhaps more fully than any of his contemporaries did. In besieged Berlin in 1945, Hartmann patiently wrote his *Aesthetics*. In the midst of war, he wrote his ode to beauty. Surrounded by a reality even more dreadful than that described by Tolstoy's fable, Hartmann mused about the meaning of life. And he neither exiled beauty nor forgot about the idea of limits. Without negating anything, Hartmann wrote about relearning to see reality, about beholding it in such a way that the imperceptible can appear through the perceptible, so we can

133

regain faith and live "a life in the Idea." However "successful" our escape into virtual reality may be, it will never successfully fulfill the deep need of the human heart for the realization of meaning. Our capacity to view the world through a loving gaze, as well as our experience of love for another human being, offers a far more promising path toward the resolution of Tolstoy's riddle: when we love, we find that life is full of meaning.

# 9. The Socratic Pathos of Wonder:
# On Hartmann's Conception of Philosophy[1]

*In attempting to grasp the nature of philosophy, as Hartmann ren-*
*ders it, it is necessary to consider some of philosophy's fundamental*
*orientations and assumptions. Hartmann's return to the sense of*
*wonder and the Socratic passion for philosophy helps us realize why*
*he is critical toward both continental and analytic traditions in*
*philosophy. Hartmann criticizes both the modern epistemological*
*turn of Western philosophy and its fundamental assumption that*
*we can know what good and evil are. Hartmann urges us to turn*
*away from the cognizing subject and return to reality, in order to*
*restore our trust and faith in what is. Only in that way, he urges,*
*can we orient ourselves toward wisdom and resume what he refers*
*to as "the Socratic pathos of wonder."*

Hartmann's conception of philosophy presents a singular challenge for an
interpreter, for it is not easy to say exactly what his conception of philosophy is, or why has it been so neglected after his death. With regard to the
first question, one notable problems is that Hartmann calls his philosophy
"new"—as in "new ways of ontology"—but also claims that it signifies a
return to and a revival of something old. He says, for instance, "once again
the primal passion of philosophy has become its attitude—the Socratic
pathos of wonder." It is puzzling to figure out how a philosophy can be
both new and old at the same time.

Regarding the second issue, we should first note that Hartmann's philosophy cannot be properly classified as either "analytic" or "continental."

1    Originally published under the same title in *New Research on the Philosophy of*
     *Nicolai Hartmann*, ed. Roberto Poli and Keith Peterson (New York: De
     Gruyter, 2016), pp. 313–32.

While it is becoming clearer that the choice between analytic and the continental philosophy is not an either-or, and that this dichotomy does not exhaust all possible options, the rift between these two philosophical traditions has dominated the Western philosophical scene throughout much of the twentieth century. Clarifying why Hartmann's orientation cannot be classified as either analytic or continental can bring us closer to understanding his unique conception of philosophy.

The plan for this attempted reconstruction of Hartmann's conception of philosophy is as follows: We will look at his claim that "the Socratic pathos of wonder" has become, again, a primal attitude of philosophy, and try to clarify it. Then, we will examine the analytic-continental divide and elaborate Hartmann's reasons for ignoring it. Despite some modern commentators who locate the source of this division in Kant, Hartmann attributes it to Descartes and the modern turn toward subjectivity. We will also need to travel back into the past and discuss, albeit briefly, why the Judeo-Christian tradition did not seem to influence Hartmann's philosophy; on the contrary, Hartmann seems to be opposed to some of the central tenets of the Judeo-Christian way of thinking. Finally, we will go back to the Greeks and the attitude of wonder. We will reconsider Hartmann's conception of philosophy in light of the original promise of philosophy—that it consists of love of wisdom.

## I. "A New Kind of Love"

The final section of Hartmann's introduction to his *Ethics* is called "The Modern Man." He opens it with a statement that, "if there is such a thing as an awakening of the consciousness of value, it is our time that has need of it." Such an awakening, however, "can hardly emanate from philosophy." Nevertheless, "this is a field for philosophy to explore," because "there are prejudices which only it can uproot. And there are emotional obstacles which reflection and the turning of the eye of the soul inward can meet." Philosophy, then, certainly plays the negative role of uprooting our prejudices regarding values. Does philosophy also have a role to play in "reflection and the turning of the eye of the soul inward"? It seems that Hartmann believes so, just as he seems to believe that philosophy is a form of self-knowledge.

136

Hartmann does not clarify these issues right away, but instead continues with his criticism of "the modern man," who, in his view, is not prone to reflection and soul-searching and may be even less sensitive toward the values that surround him. Hartmann is uncompromisingly critical: "Not only is modern man restless and precipitate, dulled and blasé, but nothing inspires, touches, lays hold on his innermost being. Finally, he has only an ironical and weary smile for everything. Yes, in the end he makes a virtue of his moral degradation."

Following Nietzsche, Hartmann suggests that, "what is bent on being destroyed one should allow to go to ruin." Then he makes a significant addition, which shows that his ultimate intention is not destructive but constructive: "Yet from every downfall young healthy life shoots forth." The goal of this regeneration is not the reevaluation of values, as Nietzsche suggests, but the reevaluation of life. The values are what they are, and we need to open ourselves to them, to experience the fullness of life. "The philosophical ethics of today stands under the banner of this task. It stands at the parting of the ways between the old and the new kind of philosophizing." The goal of this philosophizing "signifies a new kind of love for the task in hand, a new devotion, a new reverence for what is great. For to it the world which it will open is once more great, as a whole and in its smallest part, and is filled with treasure, unexhausted and inexhaustible."

Hartmann finishes this section, and the entire introduction, in the same prophetic tone: "The new ethics also has once more the courage to face the whole metaphysical difficulty of the problems which arise out of the consciousness of the eternally marvelous and unmastered. Once again the primal passion of philosophy has become its attitude—the Socratic pathos of wonder."

There are several points to notice here. One is that Hartmann switches from talking about philosophy in the future tense to speaking of it as if the transformation has already taken place. This would be hard to explain, unless he believes that he is already practicing philosophy in this spirit of the Socratic pathos of wonder.

Second, if philosophy has to return to a Socratic pathos of wonder, then the line between the old philosophy, that has to be—or has already been—abandoned, and the new philosophy, is not a line between the philosophy of the present or future versus that of the past. If the roots are still healthy and can be rejuvenated, the old philosophy that must be abandoned is not the entire philosophy of the past. Rather, Hartmann seems to have in mind some philosophy between the Socratic times and our own. If the title of this section is any indication of Hartmann's thought about this matter, his discontent is not only with modern humanity but with modern philosophy as well. This is a topic we will want to return to and address again, later.

Perhaps the central question to discuss here is what Hartmann even means by such expressions as "the primal passion of philosophy" and "the Socratic pathos of wonder." The latter phrase may be intended as a clarification of the former: Plato and Aristotle claimed, presumably following Socrates, that philosophy begins with wonder (*thauma, thaumazein*). This concept of wonder, together with to it related concepts of amazement and admiration, were clearly not invented by Socrates. They are already there, and part of the Homeric tradition. As Bruno Snell clarifies, "But amazement and admiration, even from Homer's viewpoint, are not of a specifically religious character. Beautiful women and sturdy heroes receive admiration, artfully wrought implements are 'a wonder to behold.' Admiration has always been widely in evidence, but the early Greeks were particularly susceptible to it. It is a response excited by things which are not totally strange to the onlooker, but merely more beautiful and more perfect than everyday objects. The Greek word for admiration, *thaumazein*, is derived from *theasthai*, which means 'to look.' Admiration is a look of wonder in one's eyes; it does not affect the whole man, as terror does. The eye lends a distance to things, it makes them into objects. With admiration of the beautiful usurping the place of terror before the unknown, the divine becomes once more remote and more familiar; it no longer thrusts itself upon man with the former intensity; the power of its spell over him is broken, and yet its presence appears more natural and convincing than before."

To come back to the roots of philosophical thinking: we can say that to wonder is to marvel at and be astonished by the complexity and beauty of the cosmos. Notice here the passive attitude that leads to philosophical thinking: "*pathos*" comes from "*pathein*," which primarily means to suffer, although it also means to feel. We suffer and feel what comes to us, what happens to us, and what amazes us. In this sense, passion and pathos seem almost synonymous: they refer to something we cannot control, something that seizes and overwhelms us.

To clarify the word "wonder" a bit more, let us distinguish it from mere "curiosity." What causes our curiosity, most of all, are novel things which usually have no deeper consequence for the spectator. Wonder, by contrast, deals with things that matter to us deeply. In fact, they matter so much that wonder can often lead to a profound self-forgetfulness as one is drawn into contemplation of the miracle of life. This original sense of wonder, which Hartmann ascribes to Socrates, is associated, in the thought of Plato and Aristotle, with "*theoria*" in its original sense: that is, in the sense of being totally involved in and carried away by what one beholds. According to Werner Jäger, "The *theoria* of Greek philosophy was deeply and inherently connected with Greek art and Greek poetry; for it embodied not only rational thought, the element which we think of first, but also (as the name implies) vision, which apprehends every object as a whole, which sees the idea in everything—namely the visible pattern."

## III. Continental Philosophy

If a reader were to see a text with the title "The Modern Man," but were not told the name of the author, they would likely assume it was a continental philosopher—perhaps someone like Karl Jaspers. If the ultimate question of philosophy deals with the position and role of humanity in the universe, continental philosophy tends to bypass the question of the nature of reality and rush to grapple with the question of human existence. In the words of one of its recent champions, Simon Critchley, continental philosophy focuses on the meaning of human existence. It treats this existence— and the problems of its philosophical understanding—as historically situated: "Philosophical problems are textually and contextually *embedded* and, simultaneously, *distanced*. It is this combination of embeddedness and distance which perhaps explains why seemingly peripheral problems of translation, language, reading, text-reception, interpretation, and the hermeneutic access to history are of such central importance to the Continental tradition."

An important implication of this insight is that central philosophical questions about the meaning and value of human life can no longer legitimately relate to the traditional topics of speculative metaphysics (such as God, freedom, and immortality). Our recognition of the essential historicity of philosophy implies a realization of the radical finitude of the human subject, together with the acknowledgement that there is no God-like point of reference outside of human experience from which our experience might be judged. It also leads to a recognition of the thoroughly contingent (and created) character of human experience. In Nietzsche's words, human existence is human, all-too-human, that is, made and remade by us. Perhaps the culmination and the most radical development of this realization is Sartre's insistence that there is no such thing as a pre-given human nature: "Existence precedes essence."

Of course, not every continental philosopher would go that far. It is important to realize, however, that—even in far less radical forms—the historicity thesis seems to imply a certain kind of nihilism, which is a decisive concept for the continental orientation. Continental philosophers think of nihilism as an unforeseen consequence of the Kantian critique of traditional metaphysics and the modern loss of faith. To quote Critchley again, "Nihilism is the breakdown of the order of meaning, where all that was posited as a transcendent source of value in pre-Kantian metaphysics becomes null and void, where there are no cognitive skyhooks upon which to hang a meaning for life. All transcendent claims for a meaning to life have been reduced to mere values—in Kant the reduction of God and the immortality of the soul to the status of postulates of pure practical reason—and those values have become incredible, standing in need of what Nietzsche calls 'transvaluation' or 'revaluation.'"

Heidegger, the most important representative of continental philosophy, reacts to this "break in the order of meaning" by changing the Aristotelian question of being as being into the question of the meaning of being: "The question of Being aims therefore at ascertaining the *a priori* conditions not only for the possibility of the sciences which examine entities as entities of such and such a type, and, in so doing, already operated with an understanding of Being, but also for the possibility of those ontologies themselves which are prior to the ontological sciences and which provide their foundations. Basically, all ontology, no matter how rich and firmly compacted a system of categories it has at its disposal, remains blind and perverted from its ownmost aim, if it has not first adequately clarified the meaning of Being, and conceived this clarification as its fundamental task."

The meaning of being, Heidegger argues, has been concealed, and can be recovered only in confrontation with its opposite, non-being. Furthermore, in order to overcome the centuries-old "forgetfulness of being," we need to focus on human existence (*Dasein*) and on what Heidegger believes is the most faithful encounter of which this *Dasein* is capable: our anxiety over death.

Although Hartmann does not usually engage in direct polemic, he has a number of criticisms not only of Heidegger but of the continental orientation in general. First, the concept of non-being is just a limiting concept that has no ontological significance; all ontological differences are articulations of being, not of the differences between being and non-being. Additionally, Hartmann insists that fear of death is the worst possible guide when it comes to finding out what an authentic life may be. Those who are filled with fear are incapable of accurately and clearly viewing life and reality as they are in themselves. Since death is something we cannot control, and should have no real reason to fear, Hartmann perceives an obsession with death as a pathological attitude and a form of self-torture.

Hartmann's second objection is that Heidegger's transposition of the question of being as being into the question of the meaning of being destroys the old ontology without offering anything positive in return. Ontology cannot be limited to an analysis of *Dasein*, for this *Dasein* is still a *Sein* (a form of being), and the question of being as being returns to the forefront one more time.

The third major shortcoming of Heidegger's approach is that it limits the inquiry to my individual being (*Dasein*) and ignores any form of social being; it seems thereby to eliminate the spiritual as a separate stratum of reality. Heidegger's anxiety over death limits us to the psychic stratum, and while his view does not necessarily ignore the personal spirit, it does rule out the objective spirit, which is the highest insight of the tradition of German Idealism from Kant to Hegel.

Fourth, Hartmann is opposed to the anthropomorphism of Heidegger's understanding of reality in terms of concealment. Reality does not hide from us in any way; being is indifferent toward being known. It is what it is, and it is revealed to us when we are open to it and grasp it. The truth is not relative to us, nor somehow historically colored. Of course, every problem may be presented in a way that reveals a certain historical bias, but the core of every problem is unaffected by its contextual wrappings. We need to go back to the ontological problems, which have their own ahistorical logic and their own essential characteristics. The contents of such questions are not arbitrary products of human curiosity, nor historically conditioned residues of linguistic expressions, but are rooted in the eternal mysteriousness of the world and its underlying order. In Hartmann's eyes, continental philosophy cannot be considered the highest and most serious form of philosophical thinking, because it leads to a relativistic view of truth which spells death to any philosophical inquiry and leads to an abandonment of genuine philosophical thinking.

## III. Analytic Philosophy

If continental philosophy is concerned with meaning (especially the meaning of human existence), analytic philosophy focuses on establishing facts and their structural interrelations (regardless of what meaning these facts and their relations may have). Analytic philosophy is more of a methodological orientation than a definitive set of views. Roughly speaking, it is a science-like and science-oriented kind of inquiry that aims at the same rigorous and systematic level of discourse. Some consider the true father of analytic philosophy to be John Locke, who in his famous *Essay Concerning Human Understanding* maintained that philosophy is an under-laborer of science, whose job is to clear away the rubbish that lies in the way of knowledge and scientific progress. As Critchley ironically comments, with this orientation "philosophers become janitors in the Crystal Palace of the sciences."

The analytic philosophers, successors to Locke, Berkeley, and especially Hume, focus on the mind and its work. What drives their ever-more scrupulous investigations of the ways in which the human mind works is the menace of skepticism. While the fundamental threat, for the continental tradition, is fear of the meaninglessness of human existence (or nihilism), the greatest fear of the analytic tradition is that we may be massively and systematically deceived in our cognitive beliefs about the world. Kant called it "a scandal of philosophy," meaning that philosophy was not able to offer a rigorous and satisfying proof for the existence of an external world. The project of the entire analytic tradition may thus be summed up as an attempt to show that our thoughts are not merely subjective mental experiences but that they also have an objective content, and that this content is capable of an analysis that is scientifically precise and systematic. Just as scientific experiments have to yield the same results whether they are conducted in the USA or in China, regardless of the gender, race, age, and personal inclinations of those who perform them, the results of analytic thinking are expected to have the same universally sustainable and objectively verifiable results. Nevertheless, because of the unavoidability of skeptical objections and the reality of diverse forms of the human fallibility, most analytic philosophers admit that our knowledge is a human—an all too human—affair, though they will not go so far as to imply that it is all just individual whim and arbitrariness.

Anyone reading Hartmann's books on ontology might initially suspect that he is also an analytic philosopher in his orientation. While continental philosophy generally tends to have a more popular appeal, analytic philosophy is usually scholastic, with an almost pedantic systematicity. A quick overview of any of Hartmann's major books would reveal a similarly systematic approach, and much in general that could confirm this impression of Hartmann as an analytic philosopher—at least for a while. As science is demanding and not always directly practical, philosophy, Hartmann points out, follows the same blueprint: "The basic problems of philosophy have always had an esoteric character. One cannot turn them around at will, back onto the beaten tracks of temporarily conditioned interests. They prescribe a peculiar path to the seeker, a path that is not for everyone. If the path has been recognized, then one merely has to decide to pursue it or to renounce any further foray. Renunciation of the path signifies the abandonment of philosophy. But the pursuit of the path is the undertaking of a task whose end cannot be foreseen."

There are, however, some major differences between the approach of analytic philosophers on the one hand, and of Hartmann on the other. Let us begin by looking at Hartmann's view of the relationship between science and philosophy. While Hartmann does not deny that their relationship can be, and in many ways is, collaborative, each discipline has its own respective fields of inquiry. For instance, all science and, indeed, all human cognition, presupposes a certain number of fundamental categories, such as time and space, form and matter, unity and plurality, quantity and quality, harmony and conflict, element and structure, and so on. These categories, which are common for all strata of real being, cannot be defined by science. They are metaphysical, not scientific concepts. Moreover, they are so basic that they cannot be verbally defined, for the rest of our experience is determined through them. What is possible, however, is their comprehensive analysis, which consists neither in purely *a priori* knowledge, nor in its purely *a posteriori* counterpart. Rather, such an analysis presupposes the whole breadth of human experience, from everyday life to the most sophisticated scientific research.

Despite his Herculean efforts to take this categorial analysis as far as possible, Hartmann recognizes that no such analysis can ever be decisively completed. While this would likely bother a scientist or an analytical philosopher, Hartmann is far more willing to recognize that the incompleteness of such an analysis is due not only to our subjective limitations but also to the ontological nature of reality. Similarly to scientists or analytic philosophers, he would grant that the real must be structured, but he deviates from them regarding whether or not this reality must be ultimately and in principle cognizable. Hartmann thinks that it is not, and that this is the case because, "Being itself is disharmonious, and conflict is the form of its being."

This important insight has an implication for the limitations of all human knowledge, scientific knowledge included. Over the last several centuries, science has advanced so much that it may appear that its progress is unstoppable and its limitations only temporal. It might even seem that all we need is more research and even better scientific instruments, for science to be able to resolve all the mysteries of the universe.

Things are not that straightforward, however. Kant already makes a distinction between temporary and permanent boundaries of human reason, and ultimately of human knowledge, which many subsequent philosophers and scientists have wanted to repudiate. Kant's recognition of the irremovable limits of knowledge is based on his identification of what he calls the "antinomies of pure reason." In Kant's view, there are only a few of those special antinomies, but Hegel's discovery of many more such antinomies, and his proposal to resolve them through a dialectical movement from thesis and antithesis toward synthesis, somewhat devaluates Kant's insight. Like Hegel, Hartmann discovers antinomies in every aspect of human experience, yet he does not admit their easy resolution through a higher synthesis. Only apparent (or pseudo-) antinomies are truly resolvable. The genuine ones never are.

Hartmann not only hints at the partial irrationality and unknowability of the real, but also intimates that the real has a fundamental recalcitrance, an indifference toward any subject's cognitive attitudes. Furthermore, he believes we must avoid an oversimplified picture of how a subject approaches the world and its conflicts. Hartmann's great merit is that, unlike most modern philosophers after Descartes, he recognizes the relevance of intuitive cognition, which is one reason, perhaps, why he is not too concerned about skepticism. The threat of skepticism, after all, has shifted the attention of philosophers from truth to justification, evidence or proofs, all of which require elaborate argumentation and the use of discursive thinking. In the case of intuitive cognition, however, if we recognize something, we do so directly and immediately, with no need for further evidence, justification, or proof. Unlike Kant, who views it as a scandal of human reason that we have not offered a conclusive proof for the existence of an external world, Hartmann's stance is that the scandal consists in our thinking such a proof is needed in the first place. The world is given, and this is intuitively obvious.

One reason why many philosophers would likely be unconvinced by Hartmann's repudiation is that we have traditionally separated rationality from other forms of human experience. This separation has become so habitual, and been insisted on with such dogmatic persistence, that most analytic philosophers commit what Hartmann calls a "correlativistic mistake." As Berkeley argues that, "to be is to be perceived," many philosophers have come to think that "to be is to be known" (or at least knowable). There is, in this framework, no cognitive object without some cognitive subject; no singular thing can be separated from consciousness, and there is no thing in itself; if any being is, it is only *for* consciousness. This mistake is the result not only of our concession to skepticism, but also of the inversion of the roles of ontology and epistemology, to which we will return in the next section.

Hartmann's insistence that no rigorous proof for the existence of an external world is necessary is based on his insight regarding the inseparability of emotional and cognitive acts. While non-emotional and rational cognition leaves the cognitive subject unchanged, emotional acts affect the subject who experiences them. Through various emotional acts we come to feel all the rigidity of the real, which gives us an immediate certainty of being itself, and instantly makes it obvious to us that no further proof of an external world is necessary. The fundamental and elementary truth about cognition is that it does not consist in any kind of making, as we have increasingly come to believe. In participating in reality, and thus becoming emotionally aware of it, we are more passive than active. We are unable to resist the force of the real which overwhelms us, and impresses itself upon us. Because this emotional awareness of the real lies at the bottom of all our cognitive activity, analytic philosophy makes a fundamental error when it attempts to separate cognitive phenomena from a larger life-nexus.

## IV. Against the Epistemological Turn

Historians of philosophy usually take it that the split that would ultimately lead to the distinction between continental and analytic approaches to philosophy occurs after Kant, who is viewed as the last great figure connecting both traditions, and the common denominator for both approaches. So what happens in Kant's philosophy that could explain this separation?

One way to present Kant's central insights is to say that his philosophy brings a simultaneous recognition that human reason is creative (even in cognition), and that this creative power is limited: we can never know what things are in themselves but can only know how they appear to us. The way I interpret what happens after Kant is that most of his successors, from Fichte and Hegel to neo-Kantians and analytic philosophers, gladly accept the first insight but are uncomfortable with the second conclusion and try to overcome it. Hartmann is among those few philosophers who are suspicious of the idea of the creative power of the human mind in cognition and who would rather emphasize its limitations.

Critchley sees Kant's legacy in a related, yet somewhat different light. He argues that Kant's transcendentalism led to two results that had earth-shattering effects. On one hand, Kant leaves a legacy of various forms of dualism (e.g., between appearances and things in themselves). On the other hand, he steers us toward a loss of faith—not just in the power of reason to close those gaping dualisms, but also in the power of God. As Kant's contemporary Friedrich Heinrich Jacobi put it, Kant's philosophy brings us to the crossroads at which we must make the most consequential choice: "Nothingness or a God." Jacobi explains: "Choosing Nothingness, [man] makes himself into a God; that is, he makes an apparition into God because if there is no God, it is impossible that man and everything which sur-rounds him is not merely an apparition. I repeat: God is, and is outside me, a living being, existing in itself, or I am God. There is no third."

It is hardly a matter of dispute that modern Western philosophy has for the most part turned away from faith and attempted to test the creative power of humanity. Critchley rightly warns that the results are unexpectedly alarming: "In denying God we risk turning the human being into God. That is, there is a Promethean temptation in Kantian and Fichtean idealism, where the human being turns into some replica of God, creating from noth-ing (it is worth recalling that Mary Shelley's novel, *Frankenstein* [1819], was subtitled *The Modern Prometheus*, where something monstrous stalks the scientific rationalism of the Enlightenment)."

Hannah Arendt is right to maintain that the Promethean (and Faust-ian) ambitions of humanity in the modern world lead to a spiritual home-lessness, which, in her interpretation, is manifested most clearly by our thoughtlessness and by the banality of evil. Even modern science is perme-ated with the Cartesian spirit of doubt and mistrust. Arendt is also right to claim that the loss of faith occurs long before Kant. Kant's philosophy—especially the Transcendental Dialectic of the *Critique of Pure Reason*—un-dermines our faith in the power of reason; the decline of our faith in God, however, is already visible in Descartes' *de omnibus dubitandum est*, "with its underlying suspicion that things may not be as they appear and that an evil spirit may willfully and forever hide truth from the minds of man."

Descartes certainly gives the sharpest philosophical expression to the spirit of doubt and mistrust, but that spirit itself had already emerged even earlier, because of the collapse of the medieval worldview. That worldview was undermined by a series of geographical and scientific discoveries, and perhaps even more by the internal crises within Western Christianity that led ultimately to its separation into Catholicism and Protestantism. What the Protestants protested against, and what they wanted to reform, was the corrupt Church that claimed the right to interpret, dogmatically, the mes-sage of the gospels. By rebelling against the ultimate authority of the Pope and claiming that it is the right of every believer to interpret the Bible in his own way, reformers like Luther and Calvin took their personal opinions and even their feelings as a basis on which to rebuild the entire structure of religion and their view of the Christian way of life.

This subjective turn of the Reformation opened the Pandora's box of modernity, releasing its most troubling question: Can we demonstrate that what seems subjectively apparent is true not only for the individual but also objectively and even absolutely? This question of the possibility of movement from subjective certainty to objective truth is also the central theme of Descartes' philosophy. In his effort to respond to the challenges of skepticism and secure the edifice of scientific cognition, he uses methodical doubt in an attempt to demonstrate that what is subjectively apparent has to correspond to objective states of affairs.

It is less important for our purposes to figure out whether, or to what degree, Descartes succeeds in his effort. What matters for us is that Descartes reoriented the entire philosophical enterprise from what Hartmann calls "*intentio recta*" toward "*intentio obliqua*." Following this Cartesian subjective turn, philosophers began to focus on the subject and its subjective states of mind. In terms of the philosophical disciplines, this entailed prioritizing epistemology and philosophy of mind over ontology. Hartmann laments that soon after Descartes—more precisely, after Leibniz and his follower Christian Wolff—ontology falls into a deep sleep, and this is where Hartmann thinks modern philosophy veered off in a radically wrong direction.

To explain Hartmann's technical distinction between *intentio recta* and *intentio obliqua*, allow me to use a non-philosophical example. Consider this little "poem" by Mechthild of Magdeburg, who lived toward the end of the Middle Ages (roughly 1207–1285):

"A fish cannot drown in water.
A bird does not fall in air.
Each creature God made,
Must live in its own true nature."

We are the only species that gets confused about what our true nature is; it does not happen to fish or birds, or any other kinds of living beings. This confusion has both positive and negative aspects. The positive aspect is that our confusion may guide us toward further and deeper examination of our nature, and toward expanding the boundaries of what is possible for us as a species. The negative aspect is that in this search for the new and better we can easily be misdirected, even lost. This, Hartmann believes, is precisely what happened during the era between the fourteenth and the seventeenth centuries: the many sweeping changes and radical discoveries of that time period made human beings dizzy and uncertain. Metaphorically speaking, these changes enticed us to turn our gaze away from the goals we were trying to reach in the real world [*intentio recta*] and shift our attention toward the steps we are making [*intentio obliqua*].

Think about it this way: When we are first teaching a child to walk (or to ride a bicycle, or swim) and they make those crucial first steps, we have to strike the right balance in how we help them: instead of holding the child's hands, we need to stand apart from the child, yet close enough to encourage them to look at our eyes rather than down at their feet. When the child is looking down, they are likely to stumble; if the child is too focused on each step they are trying to take, they may even fall down.

Hartmann could say that the same principle can be used to describe our adult life and our philosophy. When we are so concerned about every step we are trying to make, we lose our focus on what really matters and what is in front of us. Our balance in reality, our ability to take our steps naturally, without overanalyzing our own actions, is undermined by our desire to control every step and our fear that we may fail. Like the proverbial centipede, we become paralyzed:

"The centipede was happy, quite,
Until a toad in fun
Said, 'Pray, which leg goes after which?'
This worked his mind to such a pitch,
He lay distracted in a ditch,
Considering how to run."

In such a state of mind, we may well begin to wonder if an evil demon is deceiving us about everything we believe. In such states of self-absorbed confusion, we think we need not only a rigorous proof for the existence of an external world, but also a way to overcome the sense of nihilism that permeates our daily existence.

We should liberate ourselves from the dominant fears of both the continental and the analytic traditions by turning back to the world, with trust in that world and in our ability to appreciate it.

## V. The Myth of the Tree of Knowledge

One of Hartmann's unique strengths is his ability to avoid the pressure of the "either–or" dilemmas which characterize not only Western philosophy but much of the Judeo-Christian tradition as well. Recall how Jacobi formulated the perspective of Western philosophy—and indeed the entire Western civilization—after Kant's "Copernican Revolution": "Nothingness or a God …. There is no third." In Hartmann's view, there is a third. Moreover, this third is the right choice.

It is impossible for Hartmann to choose the side of God in Jacobi's dichotomy. Cognitively, as he sees it, we simply have no ground for such a choice. Of course, Hartmann has no problem with accepting the existence of God based on faith. What bothers him are the steps that almost inevitably follow that initial act of faith. Following our almost automatic dogmatic assertions of God's existence, which, as Kant demonstrates, we can never either prove or disprove, we tend to make two problematic further moves. One is to assign to this invisible, unknowable being a kind of reality that is much greater than any we attach to real beings existing around us. This figment of imagination, frozen in place and endowed with divine perfections that cannot be questioned—omniscience, omnipotence, all-benevolence—is turned into a dead, overwhelming, and arresting figure that supposedly creates our lives and determines our being.

In the section of *Ontology: Laying the Foundations* entitled "The Nimbus of the Sublime," Hartmann exposes the fallacy of such reasoning, which is characteristic not only of religion but also of all utopian thinking (imaging a paradise that must necessarily be somewhere else, or at some other time). It is a characteristic, too, of what Leibniz termed "perennial philosophy"—that assumes the existence of an infinite, changeless Reality beneath the world of change, the same Reality that lies at the core of every human personality, and that the purpose of life is to discover that reality in order to realize God here on earth. The real, Hartmann points out, is not that which lasts forever, arrested like a reflected image of Narcissus in its perfection. As Hartmann shows in his ontology, the real is that which is individual and unique, what is changeable and perishable, in the process of becoming and transforming. As Hartmann puts it: "What is valuable in life cannot last because it is real. If it did last, it would not have for mankind the kind of luminosity that outshines all else."

The choice not to designate God as the most real Reality does not necessarily imply the choice of Nothingness, as Jacobi's dichotomy would suggest. Nor does it imply that we humans should attempt to assume the role of gods ourselves. But a lack of intellectual modesty and self-knowledge can incline us toward such either-or thinking is. In his *Ethics*, Hartmann illustrates this through his criticism of "the myth of the tree of knowledge," which is one of the foundation stones of Judeo-Christian ethics. While Adam and Eve were still in the Garden of Eden, the serpent pointed to the tree of knowledge and prophesized: "In the day ye eat thereof, then your eyes shall be opened, and ye shall be as gods, knowing good and evil." And man, comments Hartmann, "albeit cheated out of innocence and happiness, believes. To this day he thinks that he knows what good and evil are. He believes this so firmly that even the most critical thought has fallen a victim to the great deception."

The serpent's prophecy, insists Hartmann, is "the great deception." Against the insistence of Augustine, and later Luther and Calvin, Hartmann points out that sin has not opened humanity's eyes; on the contrary, we have become even more confused as to our true nature. Not only have we not become gods; we have never even properly learned what good and evil are. This whole obsession with sin has, in fact, undermined humanity's faith in our existing world and made us feel spiritually homeless. An especially important fact, for Hartmann, is that this obsession with sin has also blinded human beings to "the glory of the imperfect," the glory of this life and of this world. Hartmann believes that instead of dreaming of heaven, a paradise remote in time or space, and instead of obsessing with sin and casting suspicion on the serpent, or on ourselves, we should learn to look at the real world again. He wants us to realize that, as imperfect as we all are, "there is something good in everyone. And it grows with the exercise of [faith] and through encouragement. It languishes through lack of appreciation. Faith can transform a man, toward good or evil, according to what he believes. This is its secret, its power to remove mountains."

## VI. Restoring Trust and Faith

Hartmann's philosophical project aims at the rediscovery of and renewed appreciation for reality. And the first step in this rediscovery of reality, he believes, must be a renewal of ontology. But why, exactly? What is so important about a return to ontology, this forgotten and abandoned discipline?

Hartmann offers two reasons. We must return to ontology, first, because all fundamental metaphysical questions are of an ontological nature and ultimately reducible to the question of being as being. Just because these questions have been neglected, ignored, or misinterpreted for so long does not mean that they have necessarily been resolved, eliminated, or negligible. For example: speaking of the distinctions between real possibility, essential possibility, and logical possibility, Hartmann comments that, "It is of no use to ignore such things because they seem formal and meaningless; one cannot overlook the consequences, and one cannot see in advance how disastrous it is if one loses one's interpretation right at this initial crossroads."

The second reason for the renewal of ontology builds upon the first. The contents of metaphysical questions are neither accidental nor an arbitrary product of human curiosity; they are rooted in the eternal puzzlement of the world and its structure. We are destined perpetually to raise these questions, and only through their systematic consideration can we prepare "the path for a well-grounded philosophy of humankind and creative action."

"The eternal puzzlement at the world and its structure" directs us again toward Hartmann's vision of philosophy as the "Socratic pathos of wonder." Let us use this opportunity to mention a few other steps, scattered throughout Hartmann's vast opus, which will assist us in moving in this direction.

We have already mentioned the significance of trust, without which the Socratic pathos of wonder would be impossible. Instead of the existentialist's *Angst* and the Heideggerian "fear of death," Hartmann proposes that we build our attitude toward reality on the open-mindedness and receptivity that arise out of trust and faith. We have sufficiently indicated that, although Hartmann occasionally uses "trust" and "faith" as nearly synonymous, they do not have any kind of narrowly religious connotation, in his worldview. Hartmann understands trust and faith in the Greek way, rather than in the way we are accustomed to understand them in the Judeo-Christian tradition. As Bruno Snell explains, "Our notion of faith or belief always allows for the possibility of disbelief; this is true in the world of ghosts, but is especially valid on a higher religious plane. 'Faith,' the *credo*, requires as its opposite a false belief, a heresy; it is tied to a dogma which people must either attack or defend with their very lives. All this was foreign to the Greeks; they looked upon their gods as so natural and self-evident that they could not even conceive of other nations acknowledging a different faith or other gods."

For Hartmann, the spiritual categories of trust and faith are of utmost importance for the full development of our humanity. In his words, "The ability to trust is spiritual strength, a moral energy of a unique kind. Its foundation is not experience, not previous testing. For it is only by showing trust that a man can be tested; and doing so presupposes that spiritual energy. Faith exists prior to experience. It alone is the foundation of genuine trust." To clarify that trust and faith are foundational for our overall orientation in reality, he adds: "In life there is always something to which a man can look up. The upward gaze is not a result, but a cause. It does not arise out of comparison, but itself selects the points of comparison. In the ethos of upward gaze all reverence and awe have their basis, as everyone who is morally unspoiled proves by his reverence and awe for real worth and merit, for antiquity or for persons in positions of higher responsibility."

This upward gaze can be partially articulated in terms of foresight, by which Hartmann understands a human capacity to look forward in time, to foresee the future and prepare for it beforehand: "Foresight is the intuitive vision in man; in its highest power, it is prophecy. Prevision makes him move forward, conscious of his goal. Man does not live in the present alone. He belongs to the future. And the future belongs to him—within the limit of his prevision."

Notice how Hartmann views this cluster of concepts including seeing, perception, vision, and intuition as especially important. A sense of wonder is not an intellectual process, even though it leads to intellectual attempts to grasp the real. Wonder depends on seeing and on something appearing to us; a sense of wonder is possible only when the given seems to allow the appearance of something that in itself is not given. The facts that analytic philosophy (and science) tries to establish may be necessary, yes, but they are not sufficient in themselves for a philosophical grasp of reality. Nor is Hartmann talking here about the meaning of facts, which continental philosophers tend to search for. Again, Hartmann believes there is some third alternative which will bring us closer to the true nature of philosophy, and thus also bring us, indirectly, to an understanding of our true nature.

To articulate what this third alternative is, let us return to the original promise of philosophy: philosophy as love of wisdom. Wisdom is not the same as factual knowledge, and Hartmann tries to distance it from any overly intellectualistic reading, such as the interpretation offered by Aristotle. Yet, wisdom has only peripheral contact with the intellectual values of truth and knowledge. While truth and knowledge are important in our instrumental reasoning concerning the means we should choose to obtain some desired ends, they do not, themselves, touch the essence of wisdom. If anything, wisdom deals more with selecting the ends than with the question of means. Aristotle's conception of wisdom in terms of *dianoia* is thus a mistake, because it pushes wisdom away from the real world and toward "contemplative self-indulgence." In contrast to Aristotle, Hartmann emphasizes that, "in the practical significance of wisdom there is a complete rapport with the world, a sensing of everything which contains value."

Again, we notice a visual element, directly related to values, which Hartmann connects with a "cultivated taste" that can be directed toward our perception of the fullness of life and an appreciation of everything of value. Wisdom is the penetration of the valuational sense into life, into every action and reaction. Wisdom is an ethical spirituality that dominates a person's entire life and allows one not so much to discover meaning but to bestow it. In Hartmann's memorable words, "For the wise man the intuitive grasping of the situation is in part determined by this wider perspective, by that of the Idea. The understanding of the significance of a situation depends upon the perspective in which it is seen. The larger the perspective, the deeper the insight into the situation. Ethical divination is the bestowal of meaning. For at bottom it is the living sense of value—but obscure, foreboding, not yet clear as to content. With a thousand tentacles the wise man reaches out beyond himself and his own limited understanding; he does not live in what he already knows of himself, but always a span beyond. This is the strict meaning of *sapientia*."

When Hartmann talks here about the "Idea," this is a translation of the Greek word "*eidos*." Although this word was "canonized" by Plato, it was well-established as a term long before he used it in his philosophy. In Homer, for instance, it means "what one sees," "appearance," and "shape" (normally of the body). It should come as no surprise that Hartmann returns to *eidos* in his monumental *Aesthetics*, where he examines the phrase

154

a "life in the Idea." Many who speak about art use this expression to mean "creation out of ideas," and interpret this as an active process of formal beholding of something that lies over and beyond all real existence. According to this view, an artist brings into the world, through their work of art, something that never was before.

Hartmann's entire aesthetics is an attempt to repudiate this view of art. As he puts it, "The artist is not burdened in this way. He realizes nothing at all; he only lets appear, only represents."

More interesting for our purposes is Hartmann's view that, "The ethical man leads a life in the Idea no less than the artist, likewise the statesman, the practically effective men of all kinds, as far as they survey only what is beyond the given." The point of Hartmann's view is that a "life in the Idea" is a human way of being creative, not by creating *ex nihilo*, but by letting something appear, and by our appreciation of it. He emphasizes that a life in the Idea consists, not in turning away from real life, but in being fully absorbed into it. In the remarkable conclusion of the *Aesthetics*, he continues to articulate this thought: "This power is a purely spiritual one, the power to enlighten and to convince in places where no demonstration and no philosophizing ever could convince man; indeed the power to direct the gaze upon what is to be beheld—in the Platonic image, to execute the act of *metastrophe* [conversion]. For that is decisive. And just for that reason, so much in human life depends upon our living, alongside of all actuality, a 'life in the Idea.' We can do that, because we possess the power of aesthetic beholding."

Should Hartmann also have not added that we can do that insofar as we are lovers of wisdom—insofar as we are overcome by the primal passion of philosophy, the Socratic pathos of wonder?

## 10. Philosophy as the Wisdom of Love[1]

*In this essay I argue that love should play a central role in philosophy and ethics. In the past, philosophical practice has been too narrowly defined both in terms of theory and explanation. Although unquestionably important, these do not belong to the very core of philosophizing. Philosophy is primarily a way of life, centered on the soul and the development of our humanity—in its most diverse aspects and to its utmost potential. For such a life to be possible, love must have a key role and philosophy should be understood not in the traditional sense as "the love of wisdom," but in a new way—as the wisdom of love.*

Why does love play such a peripheral, virtually irrelevant, role in philosophy? Is it because of the way we practice philosophy? Or because of how we understand love?

The original meaning of the word "philosophy" is love of wisdom. But the way philosophy has been practiced for centuries hardly seems to leave room for wisdom. And if philosophy is not about wisdom, love seems to play no role in it either. What is wisdom, then? And how can love begin to play a relevant role in philosophy again?

## I. Man and His Soul

Wisdom is concerned with a general understanding of what it means to be a human being and live like a human being. Against Aristotle's overly intellectualistic interpretation of wisdom, which distances it from the world of lived experience, I interpret wisdom as having to do with our fundamen-

1    Originally published under the same title in *Ethics and Bioethics*, 7:2017, No. 1-2, pp. 75–84.

tal moral commitment: it is a primal moral disposition, a commitment of a person to the richness of life in general, including one's own life and the lives of others. If society believed wisdom to be of crucial importance, then philosophical anthropology would have become the central philosophical discipline. Yet a proper philosophical anthropology, that is, philosophical anthropology as a normative discipline, has not yet been developed. Instead, humans are studied as if they were social animals or machines.

While many philosophers have contributed some insights to the establishment of philosophical anthropology as a philosophical discipline, it could be argued that the most significant contribution has been made by Kant. He insists, as few others do, that the question: "What is man?" is the ultimate question of philosophy. Furthermore, he states that the other three central philosophical questions: "What can I know?" "What ought I to do?" and "What may I hope?" all reduce to the question: What is man? This question is ultimate not because it ought to lead us to some definitive theoretical insight, but because it should make us realize who we are as well as open our vision to what we could, and perhaps should, become. Kant's implication, then, is that while philosophy must involve thought and theory, it should not be limited to them. Philosophy must include an active attempt to realize the envisioned ideals of humanity; it must integrate values, thoughts, and action. As Kant emphasizes, a genuine philosopher is the one who teaches wisdom through doctrine *and* example.

It is significant, however, that this "ultimate" question is raised by Kant only in his lectures on logic and never in any of his three *Critiques*. It is also important to recall that, despite being a prolific writer, Kant nowhere offers an answer to what he pronounces to be the ultimate question of philosophy. Most importantly of all, like other modern and post-modern philosophies, Kant's philosophy provides little sufficient ground for a comprehensive understanding of the nature of humanity; nor does he explain how wisdom should order human life. This is indicative of the peripheral role of love in his philosophy.

Kant asks: What is man? Posing the question in this way reveals a few important points. In Kant's opus, and in Western philosophy in general, the question of humanity and human nature is raised within the framework of a body-soul dualism. For Kant, this is not just a narrow question of the relationship of an individual body to an individual soul. On the most general and universal level, all being has been divided into the world's body and the world's soul. The world's body is the visible and tangible stuff "out there," Descartes' "*res extensa*" (extended thing). The world's soul is composed of the immaterial forces and divine energies that move invisibly, "in the wind" as it were. The words for *wind, soul,* and *breath* co-mingle in virtually every Indo-European language, which only adds to our confusion about what the "world's soul" could really be.

Is the soul a thing? Since we think in terms of nouns, we tend to conceive of it as a thing. Yet it is more like a non-thing. Rather than treating it like Locke's "*tabula rasa*" (blank slate), we can designate the mystery of the invisible soul-force by means of the Greek word for wind and breath: "*pneuma.*" Even though it is also a noun, *pneuma* suggests a movement and thus a verb, rather than something static and unchanging, which we usually associate with nouns and with things.

For the last four centuries, we have followed the lead of science in our attempts to understand the world (another noun word) and the things of which it is composed. In the words of William Blake, our entire culture has fallen into "a single vision and Newton's sleep." Science works because the things we dissect are visibly "out there," either to confirm or to contradict our thoughts about them. Science also works because it is based on thoughts and hard evidence, rather than on emotions, intuitions, or insights. It works because it can approach things from the outside and probe their internal structure.

By its very nature, the soul poses a different problem. The soul, by its nature, cannot easily be probed from the outside, at least by means of a science-like approach. Both rational thoughts and scientific experiments seem to bounce off the soul, without grasping what it is. Yet the internal feelings, intuitions, or insights on which we depend for an inside-out realization seem unreliable when brought before the bar of science. We are thus unable to have knowledge of the soul in the same way in which we can have knowledge of the body.

There seem to be only two ways of solving this impasse. We can either deny the existence of the soul altogether, or we can turn it into a thing, and, with renewed vigor, approach it the same way we analyze other things belonging to the world's body. The first tactic does not work, because despite all efforts to get rid of the soul, it resurfaces again not only in religion but also in arts and individual experiences. The second approach, however, has become dominant in modern philosophy. The father of modern philosophy, Descartes, did not say: "I have a soul, therefore I am," nor "I care for my soul, therefore I am," but "I think, therefore I am" and "what I think about and what I am is a *res cogitans* (a thinking thing), the thing we now call the mind." The thing we call the mind can be analyzed almost, though not entirely, in the way in which material things "out there" can be dissected: from outside-in, without emotions, in terms of quantifiable and objectively observable properties (of the brain). Thus the world's soul is treated as part of the world's body, just as an individual soul can be regarded as part of an individual body.

Bodies have no need for wisdom; they need to be pushed around, manipulated, and controlled. Their relationship is causal and mechanical, not teleological and intentional. Since love does not lead to control and domination, and since it is not an instrument of knowledge—it even appears to stand in the way of objective knowledge—love largely disappears from modern philosophy. It simply has no role to play in our attempts to understand the world's body as a whole, nor does it seem able to contribute anything to our philosophical attempts to answer the question: What is man?

## II. Ethics and the Role of Love

A window of opportunity remains open, which is why we must look to ethics. Ethics, as a philosophical discipline, deals with the behavior and attitudes of human beings toward themselves, and toward each other. And understanding love is important if we wish to understand how we relate to ourselves and to each other. Love, then, it would seem, should play a prominent role in ethics.

But even if it should, it does not. Modern ethics is mostly a morality of conduct. While its two most popular schools of thought, utilitarianism and consequentialism, do not exclude love from their considerations, love nevertheless plays no significant role in either. These two (closely related, although not identical) theoretical approaches to ethics emphasize usefulness and consequences. Insofar as love can be useful, or lead to beneficial results, it can contribute to the realization of something good. But this contribution is accidental. Love can just as well lead toward harmful relationships, or result in suffering, jealousy, and other undesirable outcomes.

Kant attempts to build an ethical theory on benevolent intentions and moral grounds alone. Yet insofar as his system is developed as a deontological ethics focusing on duties, obligations, the moral law, and the categorical imperative, it rules out the possibility of allowing love any significant role. Love can never be a duty. Nor can it be commanded. Insofar as love is understood as an emotion, it is one of the inclinations Kant wants to exclude from his ethics. He wants ethics to be rationally founded and resemble mathematics as much as possible.

Despite such views that sideline the role of love, Kant begins his ethical theory with the claim that good will is the only unconditionally good thing in the world. Good will is understood in terms of good intentions, and is akin to love, broadly understood. Thus, the door for love to have a role in ethics is not entirely closed. The language of good will is the language of benevolence, of care for our own affairs and the affairs of others. Will—good will even more so than will in general—directs us toward what we earlier called the world's soul. And the soul is essentially dealing with movement, with desire, with intention. Yet Kant does not see it that way. He ties the will to reason—practical reason, to be precise—and treats it as something akin to the intelligence used in our dealings with the world's body. Although Kant claims the supremacy of practical over theoretical reason, his ethics neglects to consider the loving care and concern one human being may have for another.

Kant is so much under the influence of Newton's ideas about the laws of nature that he tries, analogously, to establish laws of morality. Even when parallelism is not understood in such unadulterated terms, the modern ethics of conduct is conceived in terms of fundamental principles and rules. Kantian ethics is further understood in terms of the gap between "is" and "ought," and in terms of actions that can be determined as right or wrong.

Hannah Arendt contributes significantly to our understanding of how misguided this ethical orientation can be. Arendt famously coined the phrase "banality of evil" in her response to the trial of Adolf Eichmann for his role in the Holocaust. It was not that Eichmann did not understand ethical rules and principles (including Kant's categorical imperative). Nor, more importantly, was it that he acted from malevolence (or ill will). Rather, Eichmann was a thoughtless bureaucrat, someone who functioned as a cog in a powerful machine and simply followed orders from anyone above him in the hierarchy.

Arendt's account of evil, and its implication for a proper grasp of love, is supplemented by Tzvetan Todorov and Erich Fromm. Through his analysis of moral life in the German concentration camps, Todorov comes to the conclusion that the Holocaust was a manifestation of two serious problems of the contemporary world: depersonalization and fragmentation. By focusing almost exclusively on the world's body, we turn the whole world into something soul-less, value-less, and meaning-less. The next step, which Todorov believes occurred in the twentieth century, is the transformation of that soulless, value-less, and meaning-less creature into an internally divided being. Just as there is a split between the body and the soul, there is, also, a fragmentation of human mental capacities. One and the same person can be indifferent to the murder of the thousands of innocent people yet be moved to tears by a piece of music, or the death of a pet canary. Such fragmented personalities are not perturbed by genocide because the victims are not thought of as human beings but as things. They are depersonalized and treated as statistical units and numbers, mere bodies. What matters to them is whether the quota of these "things" sent daily into concentration camps satisfies the orders given by superiors. They do not care about the experiences of these people in the camps or the reasons why they were sent there in the first place.

In opposition to the ("masculine and rational") ethics of principles, followed by the organizers, administrators, and guards of concentrations camps, Todorov recognizes a different ("feminine and sentimental") kind of ethics among the inmates, the ethics of "sympathy." This ethical attitude focuses on care and sensitivity, which leads us back not only to Kant's good will, but also to love in a broad sense.

In an attempt to understand how the Holocaust was possible, Fromm coined a distinction between "*necrophilia*" and "*biophilia*." The depersonalization that Todorov observed in the concentration camp has become a prevailing fact of life in our civilization, although in less drastic and obvious forms. Life is always dynamic, like the "windy soul of the world." It continually brings changes and transformations. Dead things, by contrast, are static, unemotional, and indifferent. When we turn living beings into dead things, or treat them as such, it is often because they are easier to manipulate and control that way.

Fromm dissociates biophilia from the controlling and hoarding tendencies of modern humanity, and from our obsession with the supposed sacredness of material goods. He relates biophilia to a productive orientation of character. This creative orientation manifests itself, not in the fabrication of new things, but in loving interaction with others, in a sense of brotherhood with everything alive. For Fromm, love of life is the foundation of all positive values. The person who loves life is attracted by the process of growth in all spheres of life. Such a person prefers to construct rather than to retain. A biophile wants to mold and influence by love, reason, and personal example; they will not act by force, neither by mutilating bodies and poisoning souls, nor by the bureaucratic manner of administering people as if they are things.

The banality of evil that Arendt talks about is the banality not only of thoughtlessness, but of indifference. Just as the opposite of goodness need not be malevolence, the opposite of love need not be hatred. Indifference—insensibility, apathy, a lack of concern and interest—can be far more deadly for love than hatred is.

It is possible for people to be evil and spiritually dead even if they violate no moral law and entertain no malevolent intention. This is why the dominant ethics of principles needs to be redirected. Herein lies a possibility of opening a door for love to play a significant role in ethics and in our understanding of what it means to live like a dignified human being.

But where should we look, in our philosophical ethics, to open this door?

I believe that the past holds the key for understanding who we are, what our nature is, and how we should live. And when, as Westerners, we look at the past, we usually return to the two sources that shape us culturally: Christianity and ancient Greece. In the Christian tradition we find compassion for the suffering of our neighbors as the foundation of ethical behavior. Of course, compassion alone is not sufficient to cover the whole range of ethical behavior. But in this tradition we also find the love of God, insofar as God is understood as the highest value and outside a purely human framework. This gives us a measuring stick for who we are—a point of reference and a sense of identity.

In the Greek tradition the emphasis was on *eros*, the predecessor of what we now oversimplify and understand in terms of romantic love. We also recognize there the focus on virtue and on becoming as virtuous as one can be—as excellent as we can be as human beings. Alasdair MacIntyre revives our interest in this tradition and calls it the "ethics of virtue." Unfortunately, his focus on virtue unnecessarily narrows what the Greek tradition was about. A more congenial interpretation of this tradition may be found in what Richard Taylor calls the "ethics of aspiration" (which also squares well with Fromm's *biophilia*). This ethics of aspiration can serve as our umbrella concept for understanding not only of how love can play a role in philosophy, but—more importantly—how it can lead to a fuller understanding of how to live as human beings.

## III. On the Nature of Love

Love is an enormously complex phenomenon. The ancient Greek tradition distinguishes between *eros*, *storge* (familial-type love), *xenia* (stranger love), *philia* (communal and friendship-based love), and *agape* (self-sacrificial and even unconditional love). The Christian tradition emphasizes love of one's neighbor (merciful love) but does not neglect love of oneself ("Love thy neighbor as you love thyself.") and love of God. More recent authors speak about romantic love, love between parent and child, brotherly love, erotic love, self-love, love of God, and love of the world. What could all these manifestations of love have in common?

We can come close to answering this question if we can get rid of some of the typical misunderstandings about love. Perhaps the most damaging of these is the belief that love is an irrational, irresistible passion, and that we have no control over whether we feel it, or over how long and with what intensity it may last. Especially in its erotic-romantic versions, this irrational passion has also been tied to finding the right object and falling in love. Freud goes even further, by trying to "naturalize" love and reduce it to sexual instinct and desire for sexual satisfaction. He contrasts love as a biological-instinctual drive with the civilizational drive that wants to control, repress, and sublimate this libidinal energy for the sake of social order and stability.

Although Freud is wrong in taking libidinal energy as the main motivator behind all we do, he is right to point out that love is not a thing. We use a noun to talk about it, but there is nothing static and thing-like about love; love is not a piece of the furniture of the world's body. Due to love's energy and drive, many who criticize Freud talk about love in terms of action; they speak about benevolent action, or, more often, use a verb to express the presence of love (e.g., I love you). This approach to love is still misleading. Love is not an action of any specific, or even a specifiable kind.

Running is an action; it is clear what it involves. Helping others, say by bringing them food or medication, is also an action, but it can be done without love. What we still do not sufficiently understand is that love is concerned far less with the "who" and the "what" than it is with the "how." Love is better understood as an adverb than it is as a noun or verb. We can come far closer to grasping the essence of love when we emphasize, not a particular person or a particular action, but a way of acting. Whatever we do, we can do lovingly. Love essentially deals with how we relate: to ourselves, other people, and the world as a whole.

The second important point is that love need not be irrational. Insofar as it deals with the "how," love is an attitude and an aspiration, which we can consciously and systematically develop and practice. Fromm makes a good point when he speaks about "the art of loving," and claims that such an art relies on care, responsibility, respect, and knowledge. He furthermore correctly emphasizes that the mastery of this (and any other) art requires discipline, concentration, patience, and making the mastery of the art our supreme concern. There is no direct way of learning the art of loving, just as there is no direct way of becoming happy; it is something that can be mastered and practiced indirectly. We become the practitioners and masters of this art by developing a loving personality and building a productive and creative character.

We can now reaffirm that love has far more to do with the soul than it does with the body. Since we do not know how to deal with the ambiguities of the soul—the soul of the world, or our own—it is not surprising that we have been confused about the nature of love, nor that love has played such a negligible role in modern and post-modern philosophy. Even if we keep deceiving ourselves that we can reduce thinking to a function of the world's body, it is more difficult to sustain a similar illusion about love. However popular and widely admired, Freud's attempt to reduce love to sex is a clear failure. Despite what Freud believes, very little about love can be reduced to sex, and much about love has nothing to do with sex at all.

## IV. Reaffirming the Role of Love in Ethics

If love is a matter of the soul, and loving is an art that must be mastered and practiced, what is the relevance of love for ethics?

If love is a matter of the soul, it is connected with that movement we call will, desire, or intention. As such, love must be relevant for any ethical theory that recognizes the core of ethical values in the will, motivation, or intention. This, of course, would eliminate all versions of utilitarianism and consequentialism, but this need not worry us much. As Hartmann argues, utilitarianism and consequentialism are not, strictly speaking, ethical theories. If an ethical theory is possible only under the condition that an absolute or intrinsic good exists, then utilitarianism and consequentialism are not ethical theories, because they deny the existence of such a good. Both utility and good consequences deal only with relative good. What is useful is useful for one purpose but not another. Good consequences are good in relation to one expected outcome but not another.

The main reason utilitarianism and consequentialism are so widely accepted is not due to their inherent ethical merits. It is rather because they capture what Max Weber so masterfully exposed in *The Protestant Ethic and the Spirit of Capitalism*: the Calvinist view that redirects Christians from piety and compassion toward the kind of hard work and service that lead to tangible outcomes. A common assumption in modern Western civilization is that a lifetime of labor and service is proof of an individual's goodness and worth and, conversely, that all tendencies toward inaction, daydreaming, or sentimental attachments are outward signs of some inner moral flaw. Utilitarianism and consequentialism are thus not ethical theories so much as they are objective standards for practicality and efficiency.

Love has little to do with measured practicality or efficiency. By those standards, love is a useless value. Yet, as Hartmann points out, it may be precisely these useless values, as opposed to practicality and efficiency, that confer meaning on our lives. He insists, furthermore, that the central value of love inheres in its disposition, its intention. By its nature, love is affirmation, good will, devotion, and creativity, just as hatred is denial, overthrow, and annihilation. Love involves kindness and devotion, in the service of its object.

Love's ethical relevance is more apparent when we regard it this way. First, by loving something we display its value; we value what we love, in the sense of treating it as something special, or even, in certain cases, as something sacred. Second, if loving is a genuine good in itself, its value is neither instrumental nor relative. A loving attitude is an unconditional and absolute good. So, an ethical theory based on motivations and intentions should place love at its very core. Kantianism fails to do this because it shifts the focus from good will to duties, from benevolence to justice. Nevertheless, once developed, an ethics of aspiration will have love as its central and highest good.

Let us be more precise. Following Dietrich von Hildebrand, we can divide human motivations into *intentio benevolentiae* and *intentio unionis*: benevolent intentions and intentions striving toward unity. These two kinds of intentions do not exclude each other, but are nonetheless separable. In some forms of love (self-love, brotherly love, love among friends, love of strangers, and love between parent and child), we can see that *intentio benevolentiae* is of central significance. Such benevolence may be directed toward self-perfecting, or toward service to others: although moving in opposite directions, these two can be complementary. Also important is the realization that there are some forms of love—personal love, love of the world, and love of God—where *intentio unionis* is more directly important.

Are forms of love based on benevolent intentions the only ones relevant for ethics, or could forms of love based on the intention of striving toward unity be significant as well? That depends on what moral categories we are using. Clearly, good and evil are indispensable categories, but this does not mean they are the only ones that are relevant.

Following Kant's treatment of aesthetic phenomena, where he distinguishes between the aesthetically beautiful and the aesthetically sublime, we can posit, analogously, a distinction between the morally good and the morally sublime. Forms of love dealing with *intentio benevolentiae* would fall into the category of the morally good, while forms of love based on *intentio unionis* would fall into that of the morally sublime. However, before we decide whether this distinction is helpful, we need to clarify the category of the sublime.

"Sublime" refers to something great or superior. When we experience such a phenomenon, we feel overwhelmed by its greatness or superiority. The purest forms of the sublime can be found in the realms of religion and myth, but it is also found in the realms of nature and art. When it comes to manifestations of the sublime, we do not grasp it by means of a specific physical sense. Rather, we grasp it by means of the soul. We may even need to establish a certain distance from that which is sensually given, to experience something as sublime. Additionally, we need to distance ourselves from our ego: the less this type of experience is about myself, the more easily I can experience the sublime.

Traditionally speaking, the phenomenon of moral superiority is found in cases of extraordinary heroism (as presented in heroic epics), or of enormous suffering (as presented in great tragedies). But for the purposes of this discussion, we are more interested in whether some manifestations of love fall into the category of the morally sublime. I will leave any discussion of the love of God, which belongs more to the religious realm, for another occasion, and will instead consider instances of personal love and love of the world.

By personal love I mean an intense, prolonged, and unlimited love of one person for the unique personality of another. Unlike justice, which connects the surface aspect of one personality to the surface of another, and unlike brotherly love, which connects one's general humanity to the humanity of others, personal love unites the innermost depth of one human being with the innermost depth of another. Personal love is a complete giving of oneself to a relationship with another person: one soul surrenders to another and unites with them. Personal love involves an uncalculated giving of oneself without losing oneself in the relationship. Hartmann believes that personal love is the greatest moral value and the ultimate source of life's meaning: personal love "gives an ultimate meaning to life; it is already fulfillment in germ, an uttermost value of selfhood, a bestowal of import upon human existence—useless, like every genuine self-subsistent value, but a splendor shed upon our path."

Another kind of love which has a superior moral value, and which has been even more neglected by philosophers and Western civilization as a whole, is love of the world. For centuries we have been treating the world with neglect, even contempt. We behave as if the world exists to only to serve our purposes, as if it can only have an instrumental value. Love of the world implies a radically different attitude than this. As Schweitzer argues, love should be understood and displayed as reverence for life, for all living beings, including animals and plants. If this is the case, ethics should consist in our affirmation of and devotion to all life. More precisely, ethics should consist in my experiencing "the compulsion to show to all will to live the same reverence as I do to my own. There we have given us that basic principle of the moral, which is a necessity of thought. It is good to maintain and encourage life; it is bad to destroy life or to obstruct it."

As Schweitzer shows, love in general means a refusal to control, manipulate, or exploit. However, love of the world means the acceptance and the affirmation of *all* reality, not just of all living beings; it means the kind of surrender that leads to a sense of unity with the world as a whole, to peace of mind and serenity. The greatest champion of the acceptance of the world and serenity is Lao-tse, who insists that the invisible flow of energy ("*Tao*") is the root that gives birth to both the visible and the invisible aspects of the world, to both the profane and the sacred. Our task is to learn how not to block that flow of energy, but rather, to put ourselves in harmony with it, accepting the world and loving it for what it is. A disposition of serenity within ourselves, and peace with the rest of the world, is the ultimate form of love and the final wisdom of life. These dispositions may be the highest accomplishments of which human beings are capable.

## V. Reaffirming the Role of Love in Philosophy

Love, by its nature, is never mere sentimental kindness; nor is it about what is right or wrong. When understood in terms of moral sublimity, love takes us even further beyond the usual ethical categories. Love is a metaphysical and religious force that leads us toward philosophical anthropology, comprehensive metaphysics, and philosophy of religion. Or, if we want to avoid such abstract terminology, we can say that love, when understood from this perspective, leads us toward a philosophy of humanity, a philosophy of what it means to be human, to live like a human being, affirming our human place and role in the world. Because it leads us to a recognition that the cultivation of the soul is at the center of our humanity, love is crucial for a complete and fulfilling life. Love helps us recover what is best in us, the center of our humanity, and stimulates us to act from this center. Action of this sort is not labor, and its value is not due to any useful results or beneficial consequences. Love is a useless value that bestows meaning on life: the more capable we are of loving and surrendering ourselves, the more meaningful our lives becomes.

This is why we should not say: "I think, therefore I am," but rather: "I love, therefore I am." And what I am as a loving being is a developed and mature human, in the fullest sense of that phrase.

If these reflections are accurate, they point us toward a different conception of philosophy as well. In the past, we have been too narrowly focused on theory and explanation as defining our philosophical practice. Although these aspects are unquestionably important, they belong neither to the core of our philosophizing, nor to the core of our humanity, which Socrates so aptly captured in the injunction: "Care for your soul!"

The previous reflections indicate the primacy of the practical over the theoretical; not of practical reason over theoretical reason, as Kant would have it, but of the practical realm, in general, over the theoretical realm. Primarily, philosophy is a way of life. It is a way of life centered on the soul, around caring for the soul and developing our humanity—in its most diverse aspects and to its utmost potential. For the sake of our preservation and, even more, for the sake of our sanity, we need to find a way to overcome the modern fragmentation of personality and the depersonalization of the world. We must reunite body and soul, and develop an attitude toward other human beings and the world that is the opposite of our customary indifference. We have to learn how to love, and make the pursuit of the art of loving the sovereign concern of our lives. This is not a moral law or a categorical imperative. Rather, it is the expression of an aspiration, which we should dedicate ourselves to realizing.

To accomplish this aspiration, we need to practice philosophy from the inside out, rather than presuming that some imaginary value-neutral and cognitively detached point of view can miraculously lead us to an understanding of our proper place and role in reality. Philosophy should start with what is most intimate to us: that is, it should start with good will. It should be built on what makes us alive, what makes us most human—and that is love. In pursuit of love, in pursuit of benevolence and unity, we both display our humanity, and develop it toward the realization of our highest potential.

Philosophy began, originally, as love of wisdom. But in the course of its development, it has lost touch with both love and wisdom. The time has come to understand philosophy in a new way, as the wisdom of love. The best wisdom we have achieved is the understanding that love makes us as human as we can be. Thus our ultimate aspiration must be to become not only virtuous and thoughtful but also truly loving personalities.

## Postscript: Believing in Order to Act

In Medieval philosophy, two precepts were frequently discussed: "Believe in order to understand" and "Understand in order to believe." The Medieval world was dominated by the first of them. But in the modern period the second precept emerged as dominant, while the former came to be regarded as unacceptable.

Today, understanding in order to believe is so widely accepted that it hardly demands explanation. We are rational beings; thus, we need to understand not only what we believe to be the case but also how we need to act. "Believing that" something is the case is tied to reasons and evidence. Whatever cannot be justified on these terms is likely to be discounted as either outmoded superstition or sheer irrationality.

The ethic of the upward gaze is based on the first of these precepts: Believe in order to understand—and act. Here, the nature of believing is understood as "believing in ..." rather than "believing that ..." This shift is motivated by the need for a deeper understanding of what morality is and what it means to live as a human being.

To clarify: Our modern ethics is that of conduct; it teaches us what to do and what not to do. The ethic of the upward gaze, by contrast, is not an ethic of conduct. Although it deals with conduct (or else it would not be an ethic), it considers conduct as the surface level or the end product of more complex and deeper processes. Iris Murdoch directs our attention to this distinction when she remarks that, in the modern tradition, a moral agent is pictured as "an isolated principle of the will." In this tradition, "the agent's freedom, indeed his moral quality, resides in his choices, and yet we are not told what prepares him for the choices." Echoing Murdoch, we can say that the ethic of the upward gaze deals primarily with what prepares a moral agent for their choices, and determines their moral quality. And, based on such a deeper understanding of morality grounded in "believing in...", it also shows that a moral agent is no mere "isolated principle of the will."

But how can the ethic of the upward gaze convince us of this?

Responsiveness and responsibility are essential to any ethical system. To be moral is to act in the world in a way that is responsive both to what that world is like and to who we are. Our response to the world is not a camera-like process of recording what is out there, regardless of who we are and how we approach that world. One of the most important discoveries of modern philosophy is that, as humans, we tend to approach reality within a certain framework of presuppositions and values that shape both the objects we recognize and how, as moral beings, we respond to them. The values with which we approach the world are only indirectly a matter of our free choices. Hartmann compares values to the starry sky that exists independently of who we are and what our wishes may be. These "value-stars" attract us and, as stars guided sailors for centuries, guide us in the choices we make during life's journey.

And values can do even more for us. As we sail through life's stormy waters, values shine in the metaphorical sky above us, reminding us anew of what is important and, when our faith is shaken, helping to restore it. Morality, after all, is neither a human invention nor a social construct. Our moral life does not consist of simply choosing one option over the other, but of living in accordance with our deepest convictions. When our moral conflicts place us at those difficult crossroads at which it is easy to lose our way, neither our reasoning nor the evidence of our senses will suffice, on their own, to guide us. The more serious the conflicts, the more important it is to recognize what is essential for the human condition and of utmost value to us. Reasoning and evidence cannot teach us this. Such knowledge is already coded into the deepest tissues of our being; we know it in our bones.

The ethic of the upward gaze is not primarily about choices but about commitments, about discovering what we believe in so firmly that we are willing to stake much on it—in extreme situations, even our lives. The ethic of the upward gaze is about standing for what is most sacred to us and facing the word with the eyes of faith, come what may. This is the first key aspect of the ethic of the upward gaze.

The second fundamental element of this ethic has to do with understanding the nature of our interactions and the extent to which they dominate every aspect of our lives, including our choices. We can better understand why interactions and interactive processes are so relevant to ethics when we have a clearer perception of how ubiquitous conflicts are, in our lives. Hartmann rightly claims that "Being itself is disharmonious, and conflict is the form of its being." He urges us, therefore, to recognize that our moral life is lived in the midst of such conflicts and that the greatest challenges we face, as moral beings, are posed by life itself.

As completely black-or-white situations almost never occur in life, we rarely stand isolated from other human beings and reality as a whole. In the drama of the world, we are not spectators; we are participants. The modern understanding of the human person as a detached, anonymous, self-sufficient, and rational moral agent, is an illusion. And our separation of facts from values, of the real from the ideal, is equally illusory. Not separation and separateness but rather close bonds and partial overlaps characterize virtually every aspect of our nature and of the world.

Once we recognize the interactive nature of all aspects of reality, this helps us accept that life is full of ambiguities, paradoxes, and even antinomies. It also helps us see why modern epistemology, based as it is on a subject's mental representation of a distant object, is a misapprehension—as is the modern belief that the human person is some kind of self-sufficient moral agent who is free to make any choice they desire. Presence and interactions are far more fundamental than distance and representations. We are present in a world that does not exist for us, but does not exist separately from us, either. We live and act amid perplexing occurrences which inspire in us a sense of wonder.

The ethic of the upward gaze urges us not to treat that wonder as a mere intellectual curiosity but rather to deepen it into care, devotion, and love for the world. Wisdom consists in affirming the world while coping with the obstacles that the interactive processes in this world present. As paradoxes and antinomies cannot be simply resolved, our primary goal when approaching conflicts in the world is not their elimination. Wisdom consists in finding the strength and courage to bear them and still live in this world in accordance with our deepest convictions and sense of inner calling. It consists in living for what is most sacred to us, living with faith and understanding. It consists in acting in the world with the eyes of that faith.

When, in endorsing the ethic of the upward gaze, we assert that we should "believe in order to understand and act," this does not mean reverting to the Middle Ages. There is no return to the past. Additionally, the lessons of modernity—problematic and disorienting as the era is—must be incorporated into our post-modern approaches and perspectives. One of these modern insight we should not ignore is, as Kant succinctly put it, that human beings are creative, but our creativity is limited.

This double approach is not to everyone's taste. There are those who like the emphasis on creativity but ignore creativity's limitations. They dream of transforming human life into some kind of utopia, in which all injustice and poverty are eliminated—or, more positively, in which we all can live in peace and happiness. Others, suspicious of such "extreme makeovers" and "social engineering" believe our creativity should serve to improve our individual lives, regardless of what happens at the social level. According to this view, we should simply create private little pockets of paradise, sheltered from the turmoil of social life

Those who are more skeptical argue that our limitations are significantly greater than our creative capacities. What we see happening in the course of human history, they lament, is more imitation than creation. Human beings are fragile and insecure individually, and seek protection within a group. In fact, some argue, humans are happy to lose their identity, as well as their individual responsibility, and be absorbed into a collective identity by mimicking a group's leaders and popular slogans.

Since such group-life leads to mindlessness, or even, in some extreme cases, fanaticism, perhaps a more cautious solution would be to adopt what Arthur Schopenhauer describes as the "ethic of porcupines." Like humans, these animals want to protect each other and keep themselves warm, so the key to their—and ours—life together is to find the right distance: if they stay too far from each other, they remain cold and lonely; if too close, they stand in each other's way and prick each other.

The ethic of the upward gaze offers a way of admitting both human creativity and human limitations, without promising an impossible paradise or bringing us down to the level of self-interested animals. In combining realism and idealism, the ethic of the upward gaze acknowledges that though human beings are not yet what we could be, we have, nonetheless, the potential to improve. Kant suggests that the primary manifestation of our creativity has to do with becoming and developing a moral personality. Morality is not about following our wishful thinking, without regard for what the world is like; nor is it about adapting to the world, without regard for our own beliefs or commitments. Morality is, rather, a personalistic perspective on the world with which we are constantly interacting. And the main purpose of this perspective is to orient ourselves toward realizing the highest and noblest ideals of humanity, insofar as we can.

In developing this idea, Kant rightly distinguishes personality from individuality: the former is a qualitative category, the latter a quantitative one. The term "individual" refers to something given, whereas "person" designates the task of realizing one's human potential. Developing a personality is thus a life-long task, something that we should strive for with all our might and devotion, even if we never succeed in fully realizing it.

Hartmann significantly enhances Kant's conception of person and personality. Living almost a century after Kant, Hartmann witnessed an increasing and systematic depersonalization of human beings. He saw that humans were being treated as anonymous and replaceable parts of the world-machine, mere numbers and statistical units exploited in the quest of the few for greater power and profit. Hartmann's ethical approach, culminating in his conception of personality and personal love, stands in striking contrast to the growing anonymity and homelessness of allegedly self-sufficient individuals with their supposed freedom to choose how they desire to act. For Hartmann, personality is a spiritual as well as a moral category, and a person is, above all, a spiritual being. When facing others, whether moral and spiritual beings like us or various representatives of animate or inanimate reality, we should treat them with the utmost respect. As Hartmann puts it, we should treat them all lovingly. When we encounter other human beings, we should look for the best in them and regard them as capable of distinguishing truth from falsehood, good from evil, beautiful from ugly. To live like a human being, according to both Kant and Hartmann, is to follow the highest values and take the high road of morality.

When discussing personality, Kant focuses exclusively on a general idea of humanity. Hartmann, countering not only this one-sidedness but also the developing culture of reducing humans to anonymity, rightly complements Kant's account by insisting that each personality also carries within themself an ideal that is unique: our distinctness is of equal importance and equally in need of further development as our general humanity. The goal of such development is the uniqueness of commitment of values and, indirectly, uniqueness of the valuational perspective with which a man permeates his sphere in life. A developed personality carries his standards beyond all questions in himself. In following them such a person is loyal to himself. "He shows very definite and unmistakable sympathies and antipathies, for which he can give no other account than that which is to be found in their existence and their felt necessity. He sees the world, in a light of his own, as no one else sees it, in the light of his preferred values; and lives in accord with them."

As a participant in the swirl of opposing aspects, tendencies, and forces interacting in the world, personality has to assimilate and integrate such opposites. Hartmann understands personality as a being living at the boundary of the real and the ideal, as the only being of which we know capable of amalgamating their reciprocal impact. By doing so, personality enables the instantiation of values and meaning into reality. A spiritual person strives toward unity and integrity by following the values which they cannot create and which are not temporal. The capacity to distinguish truth from falsehood, good from evil, and beauty from ugliness has long been taken as an indication that there is a realm of being beyond that which is relative, subjective, transitory, and changing. These distinctions direct us toward the possibility of the ingress of the eternal into the temporal, thereby making personality the point of interaction of these two seemingly incompatible dimensions of existence.

By relying on emotional intelligence, through experiences such as love, joy, and pain, for example, we can open eternity to time. And when we do so, everything in our field of experience is transformed. In the spirit of Hartmann, Erazim Kohak develops these insights even further in his book, *The Embers and the Stars*: "As there are humans who are color-blind, so there can be humans who become blind to goodness, to truth and beauty, who drink wine without pausing to cherish it, who pluck flowers without pausing to give thanks, who accept joy and grief as all in a day's work, to be enjoyed or managed, without ever seeing the presence of eternity in them. But that is not the point. What is crucial is that humans, whether they do so or not, are capable of encountering a moment not simply as a transition between a before and an after but as the miracle of eternity ingressing into time. That, rather than the ability to fashion tools, stands out as the distinctive human calling. Were it not for humans who are able to see it, to grieve for it and to cherish it, the goodness, beauty, and truth of creation would remain wholly absorbed in the passage of time and pass with it. It is our calling to inscribe it into eternity."

The key to our moral and spiritual life, and to our distinctively human calling, is to live inspired by eternal values while interacting with the world in the dimension of time. This is what it means when we assert that we should believe in order to understand and act. And this is at the heart of the ethic of the upward gaze.

# Index